Dedication

This book is dedicated to everyone who has faced a crisis and was unsure what to do or say. It is dedicated to the often thankless role of being the voice or the face of a crisis. It is dedicated to anyone who engages in interpersonal communication and would like to improve their words, tone, and physiology in order to improve relationships. Yep. It is dedicated to everyone. Mostly, we dedicate the work and effort here to our friends and family who supported and encouraged us to make it happen.

Table of Contents

Dedication

Introduction

Part 1: Seeds

Part 2: Branches

Introduction

By Dan Stoneking

The beauty of art is our opportunity to interpret what we consume. I read Voltaire's *Candide* while I was in college. It made a profound impact on me. My take – the protagonist, Candide, follows his tutor around the world in search of all the best things. Instead, they find tragedy, violence, and heartbreak at every turn. In the end, the tutor comes to Candide to justify the journey and convince him to do more of the same. Candide pacifies his teacher but stands fast in his position that first we *must cultivate our garden.* What I have always inferred from that philosophy is that our time is better spent making what we have better, rather than looking and hoping we stumble across better things.

It is good to eat vegetables. It is *great* to grow them. It is good to be responsive. It is *great* to change the world. We are hired to plant ideas, grow programs, and make the world better. Let us dedicate some of our time to cultivating our own gardens and not 100% of our time responding to tasks and simply answering emails.

The purpose of this book is to empower strategic communicators at all levels to cultivate their own gardens before, during, and after a crisis. We have all been through a crisis or two. The next one could occur tomorrow.

This book is different. The soil is fresh. Each chapter shares unique content but with consistent attributes. Each chapter begins with **a quote or two**. I encourage you to pause and reflect on why they were chosen. Each chapter also begins with **a photograph**. In Chapter 10 you will have the opportunity to caption each one. Along the way, in every chapter, you can interpret the relationship between the text and chosen imagery. And every chapter weaves in **anecdotes, experiences and stories.** Whether you consume information textually, visually, or experientially, they are all here for you.

Once we have whetted your appetite, each chapter provides a strategic overview. The strategic level is often referred to as a **30,000-foot** view. This term comes from the approximate cruising altitude of commercial airliners. Visual learners can imagine what that view looks like. Strategy is important. It is essential. But strategy is not the complete story.

So, in this book, in addition to the strategic insights, each chapter will also include more operational and tactical pointers - the view from **three feet**. They will help to quickly transform those strategies into action at work, today and tomorrow. As C.S. Lewis realized, "A glimpse is not a vision. But to a man on a mountain road by night, a glimpse of the next three feet of road may matter more than a vision of the horizon."

This book is not intended to be a comprehensive tome about all strategic communication activities. That would be tedious to write and to read. Rather, this book explores concepts that are too often forgotten, and nuances not always taught in formal courses, with a specific lens on crisis communications. Yes, there are many chapters. But each one is noticeably short - a three to seven minute read. The chapters can be read in any order or straight from beginning to end. If you gain two to three snippets or even epiphanies from this book – and I think you will – the cost and time will be more than worth it.

Finally, this book is the result of **collaboration**. Crisis communications should always be a collaboration. In each chapter we will identify the author, either Dan or Rebecca. One features a point - counterpoint approach. Read more about us at the end of the book and you will see that we are two different gardeners, with different experiences, perspectives, and tools. Mike Stoneking designed the cover and section breaks. He also provided many of the images, formatted all of them, and provided consultation, feedback, and support from the beginning to the end.

Rebecca and I are grateful for his meaningful contributions.

Seeds

If you plant seeds every single day, you will always have something to harvest. When you nurture them with patience, determination, and dedication, they grow healthy and strong. In a healthy environment, wonderful things will happen that you can't even see at first. In this part, we will address those aspects of crisis communications that embody the soil and foundation to help you ensure sufficient water and sun for growth, while avoiding the weeds. If you tend to these basics well, and master the care and feeding, you will be ready to sprout towards greater growth.

Chapter 1   Reputation Management

"It takes many good deeds to build a good reputation, and only one bad one to lose it"
-   Benjamin Franklin

"It takes at least three 'atta boys' to overcome one 'ah shit'"
-   Al Stoneking (my dad)

Chapter 1　　Reputation Management by Dan Stoneking

Like too many teenagers, I once wrecked my parent's car. Actually, it was my Mom's car. The first car she ever owned by herself. It was a 1978 Mercury Bobcat. It was essentially a Ford Pinto, but with a different grill and more stylish interior. Oh, how she loved it. I borrowed it to go to Kingswood Regional High School for a play rehearsal. We were doing "Sound of Music" that year. It was a cold New Hampshire Saturday and when I arrived, Todd was the only other one there with a car, but many more students had been dropped off by their folks and were waiting for the school to open. Todd and I opened our doors and about six or seven classmates squeezed into each car. Then we did what seventeen year old boys do - we raced our cars around to the back parking lot to see if that school door was open. I swerved, he swerved. My car collided with a large boulder and the passenger door of the Bobcat was destroyed. Fortunately, nobody was hurt. Well, until I had to face my parents.

I was in the doghouse. The prom was a few months away and I wanted to earn back some trust so I could borrow one of the cars again and not be humiliated by my Dad driving us. While they were both away for the day, I spent several hours doing yard work, mowing, hauling away branches, laying mulch, and weeding the garden. When they returned, I showed them my handywork, hopeful for a positive response. My dad glanced around and then looked me in the eye, "It takes at least three 'atta boys' to overcome one 'ah shit,'" he said.

It took a moment to process, but it has proven true through a lifetime.

30,000 Feet

Everything that we do, or do not do, impacts our reputation. It is the foundation that impacts all communications. If the foundation is shaky or cracked, communications become tenuous at the outset. On firm and respected bedrocks of values and behavior, the communications have a positive head start. Mostly, folks tend to think about individual reputation. But agencies, organizations, and businesses have them too.

In 2023, Anheuser-Busch introduced a marketing campaign featuring transgender TikTok star Dylan Mulvaney, who promoted the company's "Easy Carry Contest" on social media.[1] As you read this, some of you may have supported the

---

[1] Everything to Know About the Bud Light Controversy, by Skyler Caruso (PEOPLE Digital)

campaign and others not, but what is indisputable is that Anheuser-Busch's reputation changed that day. And related to that change in reputation, sales dropped dramatically, people lost jobs, and customers were offended. There is no easy talking point for that. This is a stellar example to demonstrate that an organization's reputation precedes all future communications. It also highlights the aspect of reputation management when organizations must consider who's opinion of their reputation matters. In the corporate world, the answer to that is often everyone, since offending anyone can negatively impact sales.

Each year since 1976, Gallup conducts a poll of Honesty and Ethics of Professions.[2] Commonly, nurses and teachers rank high, and Members of Congress and telemarketers rank low. When I go to the hospital and a nurse gives me a shot, I never stop to question her ability to do so effectively. But when a telemarketer calls, I do not even answer the phone. In fact, teachers and nurses do not even need spokespersons, but Senators sure do. It all comes down to reputation.

It is worth noting that we can have a powerful reputation in some areas but a weak reputation in others. Your local McDonalds may have a great reputation for efficiency and even taste, while

---

[2] Honesty/Ethics in Professions (Gallup)

having a poor reputation for nutrition. Costco has a great reputation for reasonable costs and solid quality, but many customers are not too happy about having their receipt reviewed prior to exiting. In 2022-23, the Boston Celtics had a great reputation for defense and a poor one for turnovers. As a fan, I appreciate that reputations can change.

Whether in whole or in part, stagnant or in flux, our reputation remains the foundation that our branding, slogans, key messages, and all talking points stem from. Comcast Xfinity boasts the slogan, "This is easy. This is simple. This is awesome."[3] But if the customers do not enjoy the quality, service, and value, then the reputation suffers, and the words become hollow.[4]

Three Feet

Reputations are not forged in nickel; they are shaped in clay. Reputations are malleable. Crisis communicators have an obligation and an opportunity to provide counsel to leadership *before* there is a problem. Throughout my career people often asked me two common questions. What is the most important skill for a communicator to have? What is the weakest skill

---

[3] Comcast
[4] Research Business Reviews Before Buying (sitejabber)

most communicators have? Unfortunately, the answer to both questions has been the same: leadership counsel. The next time you are in a meeting and the topic makes you think, darn, that will be hard to message someday, speak up. Speak up right then. There are several aspects to organizational reputation, and you can impact each of them.

It always starts at the top. Organizations are measured by the quality of their leadership and management. Do they have experience? Do they steer the organization in the right path? Do they adapt to change? We all know the adage perception is reality. We have many opportunities to measurably improve these skills. Set up individual mock interviews for the entire leadership team. Do them individually so none of them feel put on the spot among peers. Film them and review the film with each of them. Try to do these at least once a year and certainly when new members join the team. In fact, mock media interviews should even be part of the hiring process.

In 1985, Blockbuster opened its first video rental store and eventually grew to more than 9,000 stores globally; in 2010, the rental company filed for bankruptcy.[5] They did not steer the company in the right direction nor adapt to change. Sure, the boss, the board of directors, the list is long of whom to blame. Among them, I would include the entire public relations team for the fall. We are the ones responsible for tracking and understanding public sentiment. There was ample time for them to engage in the early 2000's. And here is a simple key to success - the crisis communicator must be a member of the leadership team and not buried in the structure without a voice. Fight for that if necessary. We will dive further into that in Chapter 23, *Respect, Gravitas, and a Seat at the Table.*

Another aspect of organizational reputation is the quality of the product and/or services. These must be consistent, reliable and desirable. Have you ever driven or even been inside a Porsche? They have an impressive reputation for high quality materials. In fact, even though they are in the same category as Mercedes Benz and BMW, Porsche ranks number 1 according to consumer reports.[6] Easy job for the communicators to tell the Porsche story. Now consider Frontier Airlines, which suffers a 2/10 rating from more

---

[5] The rise and fall of the movie rental store, and what happened to the brand (Insider)

[6] Companies and Products With Outstanding Brand Equity (Investopedia)

than 3,000 reviews.[7] Imagine the board room meeting at Frontier. Low scores for Food & Beverage, Inflight Entertainment, Seat Comfort, Staff Service, Value for Money. Perhaps the communicator in the meeting could not influence the seat comfort, but some of the other issues are softballs. Staff can be better trained, especially in interpersonal communication. There are thousands of opportunities to improve the entertainment, Value can certainly be communicated better and that is the communicator's wheelhouse. Do not put lipstick on a pig when you can turn a pig into a stallion.

Frontier has three slogans: "The Spirit of the West." "Low Fares Done Right," and. "A whole different animal."[8] First, having three different taglines is confusing and they diminish each other through baffling internal competition. The first one includes the name of a competitor, Spirit Airlines. The second one boasts "done right" Are they, really? And the last one is an easy target for mockery. It sure is a different kind of animal. So here is a fun exercise to play now or do it later with your work team. Write your own slogan for Frontier Airlines. I am sure you will quickly find, especially brainstorming in a small group, that you can produce better options, in less

---

[7] Frontier Airlines Customer Reviews (Skytrax)
[8] Frontier Airlines Logo and Tagline (Logos and Taglines)

than an hour. Then go back in your mind and think about the Frontier communicators. They had the opportunity to make a more effective impact on the organization's reputation.

Fiscal responsibility, hiring the right people, diversity, social responsibility, and innovation are all further aspects of organization responsibility. Just like quality of leadership, products, and services, the communicator can impact each of these. Another exercise opportunity is to create a two column chart for your team with each of these aspects in the left column and how you as a team can impact change in the right column. Then take those ideas to the leadership team. Even if you do not succeed in four out of six, imagine the difference you can make in improving the reputation in two areas. The reputation boost will also make your job easier. You will be the one driving the Porsch.

Take a moment to assess your own reputation. Just like the organization, everything you do or do not impact your reputation. Do you know your reputation? There are countless ways to find out, including 360 peer reviews and a plethora of personality tests, along with your performance review. But a really simple one you can do with either your team or peer group is to do a simple ice-breaker game at your next meeting. Ask everyone to write down what animal they see themselves as and what animal they see everyone else as. Your results may surprise you and they will give you an opportunity to shape and adapt your behavior to earn the reputation you seek.

###

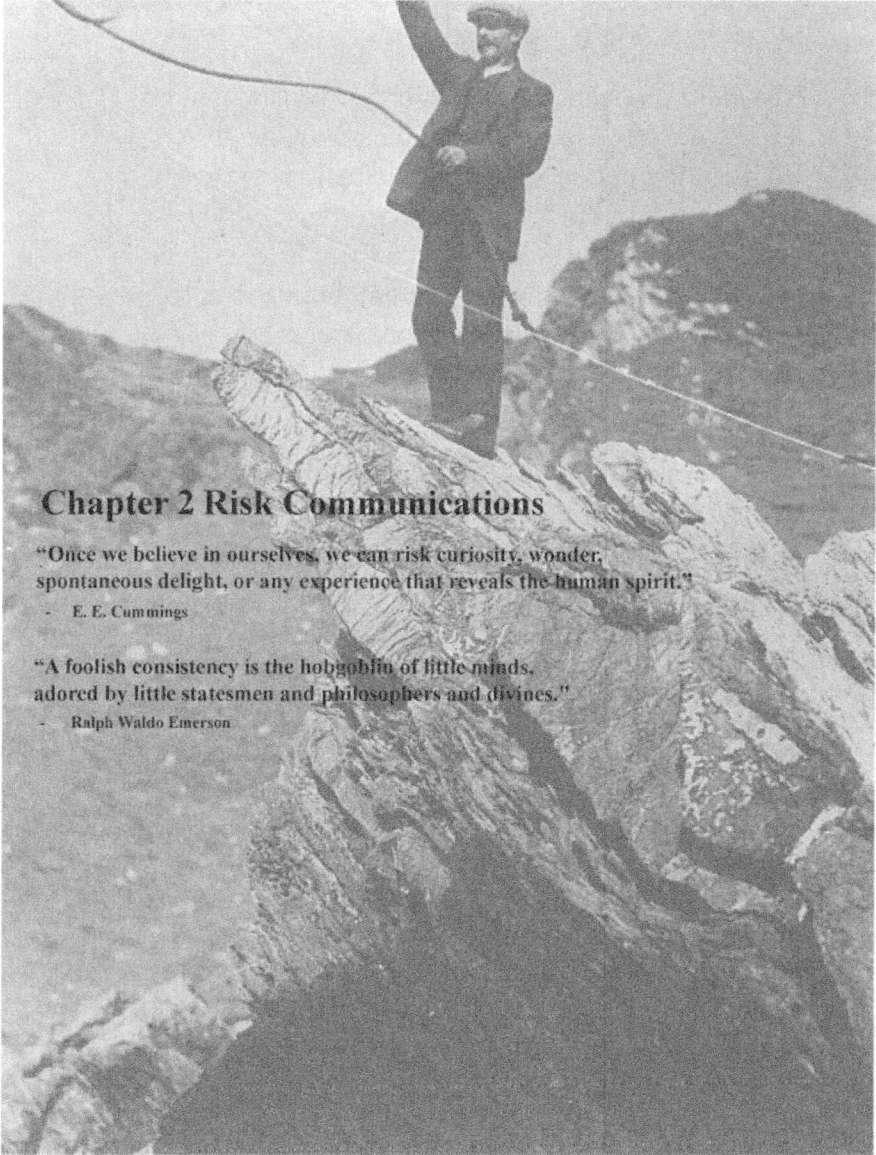

Chapter 2 Risk Communications

"Once we believe in ourselves, we can risk curiosity, wonder, spontaneous delight, or any experience that reveals the human spirit."
-   E. E. Cummings

"A foolish consistency is the hobgoblin of little minds, adored by little statesmen and philosophers and divines."
-   Ralph Waldo Emerson

Chapter 2   Risk Communications by Dan
Stoneking

Risk communications happen before, during, and
after a disaster. On that point, most would agree.
But how to conduct risk communications varies
greatly. In fact, some organizations place little to
no emphasis on risk communications. In
emergency management, risk communications
overlaps and intertwines with preparedness
messaging.

Recently, I watched a new movie on Netflix
called "Jesus Revolution."[9] Kelsey Grammer
stars as Chuck Smith, a pastor who faces a
turning point in his church. The movie, based on
real events, included a fine cast and several
quotable moments. Chuck's wife Kate (played by
Julia Campbell) only had a dozen lines, but in my
mind, she delivered the most powerful line in the
movie when she advised her husband, "The truth
is always quiet."

It struck a chord with me so fervently that I had
to pause the movie. And I thought about it for
days. It reminded me of another powerful and
parallel quote I have cherished for more than 40
years. And like Kate's line, the subtlety of this
reference may surprise you. It comes from the

---

[9] "Jesus Revolution" (IMDb)

first paragraph of Stephen King's short story, "The Body" (later retitled "Stand by Me," when made into a movie). King's observation begins and ends with "The most important things are the hardest things to say… [and stay] … locked within, not for want of a teller but for want of an understanding ear."[10]

Maybe that is *why* the truth is always quiet.

Crisis communications happen *after* things have gone wrong. Risk communications deals with things that *might* go wrong. In theory, the better we engage in risk communications, the easier it will be to conduct effective crisis communications. Unfortunately, we do not do a decent job communicating about risk. We publicize and over-promote so many loud preparedness messages like have a family preparedness plan, have a go-to bag, buy flood insurance, and more. And yet, formal surveys and studies have shown that regarding these factors there has been extraordinarily little progress, if any, statistically in more than thirty years of heavy and loud messaging.

Why is that? Are we telling the truth? Or has our truth been too quiet for lack of understanding ears, internally and externally?

---

[10] "The Body," by Stephen King (LiveJournal)

I have personally endured a flooded home. I overcame an extended power outage. I was in a building when there was an explosion. I witnessed a tornado in my path. And I have survived a 6.2 earthquake. I did not have a plan, a kit, or insurance during any of these instances. I was self-reliant.

Isn't that the truth here? Do we care if someone has a written plan if they can take care of themselves and free-up emergency responders for those less fortunate? Let me pause for critical clarity – there will always be disadvantaged, historically underserved, and disenfranchised people who need help. And we must always help them. But responders cannot always focus on them because of all the time consumed helping people who could have helped themselves, like a capable individual who simply chooses not to evacuate.

So why don't we message self-reliance as the primary message in risk communications? Internally, emergency managers at all levels of government fear the message will backfire on them. They think people will claim – that is what you are here for, that is why we pay you. Externally, it may not land on understanding ears. I get it. Not an easy transition. But if what we have been doing for more than thirty years has not been working, why not try the truth, and avoid the "foolish consistency" that Emerson cautions against. The more people are self-reliant, the less challenges there will be for emergency responders, the more they can help those truly in need, and the faster the community will recover. Self-reliance should be the message.

Self-reliance is true. In the movie, Kate also reminds her husband, "Truth is simple." It can be. It should be. But it takes courage. Self-reliance is the risk communication challenge I offer to each of you. It may be a long-term goal.

30,000 Feet

Self-reliance aside, people perceive and respond to risk in very different ways and different times. At its core, risk communications begins with how we communicate at all. Even one simple message is a complex process. The sender → crafts a message → that is filtered by his/her → experiences and environment → then it goes through all kinds of noise and interference, depending on the medium → then through the receiver's environment and experiences → finally to be decrypted into what they receive and hear.

That is a lot to unpack. A simpler version, you probably played as a kid, is the "Telephone

Game."[11]   Remember how you would all stand in a line and the first kid would be given a word or phrase and had to whisper it, just once, to the next kid and so on, until the very last kid got to shout it out and invariably it was not even close to what was started and intended. Same thing. But this time with more complex information and a wider audience.

Risk communications can and should occur, before, during, and after a crisis. Most organizations employ risk communications before, but it often has minor impact, because there is not a catalyst to garner attention and promote action. During and immediately after a disaster, the immediacy triggers different priorities. For example, it is difficult to convince someone to buy flood insurance on a random Tuesday. It resonates more after their home or business has been flooded, or that of a neighbor's.

During and immediately after a disaster, fear becomes a motivator. Fear is an important and complex psychological consideration. In some cases, a perceived threat can motivate and help people take desired actions. In other cases, fear of the unknown or fear of uncertainty may be debilitating and prevent action. The key to

---

[11] Chinese Whispers, Wikipedia

finding that fulcrum between action and debilitation is curiosity. There is an iconic dart game scene[12] in the Apple TV show "Ted Lasso" where the titular character talks to his opponent about the value of being curious. It is also valuable to be curious in a disaster. Talk to survivors and local officials. Be curious about how they feel and what they need. The balance in messaging rests among their perceived risks, their actual risks, effective preparedness measures, and their ability to relate to them. Ted won that game of darts because his opponent was not curious. He never thought to ask if Ted had even played before.

Risk communications is a constant process. It involves an exchange of information and ideas in both directions. During steady state, it is not a one-time activity, but rather a drum beat with a constant rhythm. During and after a disaster, it becomes a more focused effort, built upon curiosity, to motivate change.

Finally, in risk communications it is essential to remember the audiences. They typically fall into three categories, allies, adversaries, and ambivalent. And in all cases, whether we are discussing peanut butter, artificial intelligence, or emergency management, there are two constants.

---

[12] "Ted Lasso," YouTube

One, the allies and adversaries combined are a smaller number than the ambivalent. And two, the allies and adversaries are not the ones you want to reach anyways, since they are already rooted in their opinions. Let us use peanut butter as an example to make extreme points. No one in the industry would develop a commercial to only show at the annual peanut butter convention. Those people are already into peanut butter. Likewise, it makes no sense to have a campaign directed at people with nut allergies, because clearly, they will not be interested. So, the industry develops a broad campaign to reach out to all those who may not know or yet care how good peanut butter is on celery, or mixed with chocolate, or simply in a classic peanut butter and jelly sandwich.

Okay, silly example to make a point. So, let us bring it home to risk communications. I have seen risk communicators spend substantive time, money, and resources to develop podcasts on risk communication topics, like having an emergency plan, getting flood insurance, or the value of a preparedness kit. But who is listening? The allies. I like biking, kayaking, and playing tennis. If I came across a podcast about one of those, I might invest the time. However, I have zero interest in the mating habits of tsetse flies, so no amount of promotion could get me to tune in. Podcasts have value, but not in reaching the ambivalent. More on social media in a later chapter.

I also remember an incident, when senior emergency managers flew to Atlanta to meet with an editorial board at CNN to try and convince them to be more supportive in their coverage of disaster response efforts. Yet, CNN is an adversary here. They cover topics that maintain and increase viewership, without any allegiance to the emergency managers. In my humble opinion, the trip was a waste of time and money.

Three Feet

Given those challenges, what can we do today and tomorrow at work to make a difference? It starts with developing the message. The first steps in this stage are knowing the issues and knowing the audiences. Sounds simple, but if we take a look at our organizations, have we really done that? Sadly, I have known communicators to spend years in an organization without really knowing how the sausage is made. Picture this scenario. Your company makes widgets. Someone claims the widgets are not safe and malfunction. The communicator reaches out to the operational section. The operational section ends up writing a brief or talking points. The communicator brings that back and you publish a statement. Sound familiar? Make sense? Ask the communicator a few questions. Did they make any edits to what the operators wrote? Does the communicator fully understand widgets? Can the communicator explain the issue in their own words without notes? This drill is essential. The operator's job is to make safe and reliable widgets. The communicator's job is to demonstrate to the public that the widgets are safe and reliable. And the communicator can only do that effectively if they truly know the issue. The operator provides data; the communicator translates that into clear, concise, and compelling words.

We must know the audiences too. Are they well informed? Do they care? Are there different audiences with different agendas? Do we know who is buying the widgets and who is claiming the widgets are not safe and why?

With those core principles in place, messages should be simple, timely, accurate, and credible. They should be read, heard, and understood. They should make people feel good about the product or service. Here is an example from a highly respected company, Proctor and Gamble:

> *"Our brands are trusted in millions of living rooms, kitchens, laundry rooms, and bathrooms—and have been passed*

*down from generation to generation. We
are the people behind the brands you
trust, and we are committed to making
peoples' lives better in small but
meaningful ways, every day."*[13]

So much positivity, millions… generational…
trust... committed... better… meaningful.

Now consider this talking point from Health and
Human Services.

> *"The mission of the U.S. Department of
> Health and Human Services (HHS) is to
> enhance the health and well-being of all
> Americans, by providing for effective
> health and human services and by
> fostering sound, sustained advances in the
> sciences underlying medicine, public
> health, and social services."*[14]

Aside from it being less simple, is it accurate and
credible? After COVID, do most Americans find
this true and relatable? Do we feel that HHS has
enhanced our health and well-being? The
bureaucratic differences between the two may be
subtle, but they make all the difference. When we
hear the words "kitchen," "trust," and

---

[13] *Who We Are*, Proctor and Gamble
[14] *About Us*, U.S. Department of Health and Human
Services

"generation," we think about family and feel warm. We do not feel much emotion when we hear, "...sustained advances in the sciences underlying medicine...."

Another fun drill. Have your team try to write better talking points for both of the examples above. Improving on P&G would be impressive. Making HHS' statement better should be an easy task. After you read and discuss the submissions, ask each presenter how much research they put into each organization first. Did they ever open their websites? If all they did was put better words on paper, it is an opportunity for you to review and reinforce the first steps of knowing the issues and the audiences.

There are some basic truisms in risk communications we can begin using today if we have not already. One of them is that the average American reads at the seventh- to eighth-grade level.[15] In a disaster, with fear, safety, and other concerns competing, that drops even lower. To put this into perspective, I pulled down a random article from Boeing's website, *"Boeing Partners with the World Energy Council...,"* dated Sept 5, 2023.[16] I then pasted that article into an online

---

[15] *Top 10 U.S. Literacy Statistics,* Cross River Therapy
[16] *"Boeing Partners with the World Energy Council...,"* BOEING

text analyzing tool, called "Analyze My Writing."[17] Boeing's release was rated between a 17 and 22 grade level. I then pasted the first three paragraphs of this book's introduction that you are reading now. It was rated between a 7 and 10 grade reading level. Finally, I pasted the first stanza of the poem Mary Had a Little Lamb, which rated between a 3.5 and 6 grade reading level. We will reach more survivors and motivate more action when we can keep our messages simple. There are many tools online to analyze writing. Beyond readability, they can evaluate frequently used words, passive voice and much more. Have fun, pause this book for a moment, and put your last release through the analysis.

Another truism often used among crisis communicators, was *"created by some Vermont lawmakers several years ago, the 27-9-3 rule requires you to make your persuasive point in no more than 27 **words** within a time frame no longer than **nine seconds** with no more than **three points** discussed."*[18] I do not suggest getting bogged down in math. You may produce a brilliant solution in twenty-nine words and/or at times you may need a crucial fourth point. But it is a great exercise to develop initial messages,

---

[17] *Analyze Text for Readability,* Analyze My Text
[18] *27-9-3 Elevator Speech,* My Power People

and further supports the readability and audience understanding.

The last truism I want to share is one that I learned from Dr. Vincent Covello, the Compassion, Conviction, and Optimism (CCO) template.[19] The template follows this order. First, express sincere compassion. Demonstrate empathy for what the survivors are experiencing, their losses, their fears. Second, relay the conviction and determination you bring that will soothe and reassure audiences. Third, provide optimism, hope for tomorrow and the next day that things will get better. This is another easy drill to mimic in training exercises.

Another area to consider is outreach channels. I have had staff come to me and ask, "Should we push out a release, make an infographic, shoot a video, or post on social media?" I like to respond with a simple, "yes." The media and mediums we use should only be limited by our resources to do so. If you have the time and staff to push messaging through multiple platforms, do it. The same is true for pitching interviews. We do not have to pick television, radio, print, or internet; we can, and should, pitch to all of them.

---

[19] *A Powerful Tool for Risk, high-Concern and Crisis Communications,* Vincent Covello

I have shared here the basic steps and exercises at the three foot level. Before we leave this chapter, I want to address a valuable resource and the benefits of synchronization. There is a wealth of useful information at Ready.Gov.[20] The site has talking points separately for before, during, and after dozens of different disasters. It can be a simple cut and paste for most disasters. Ready.gov is available in several languages, and even has focused messages for different groups like elderly or pets.

For all of the messaging, truisms and resources to work, they must also be synchronized at the local, state, and federal level. If the county is engaged in risk communications about nuclear power plants, while the state is pushing cybersecurity awareness material and the federal government is promoting hurricane awareness, then they each end up competing with each other and diluting messages.

Many years ago, I worked with the Ready.gov campaign to develop monthly themes.[21] By following the calendar, local, state, and federal communicators empower each other and strengthen the messaging. My team would then create news release templates, social media

---

[20] Ready.Gov
[21] *Ready 2023 Calendar*, Ready.gov

messaging, and more that state and local officials could quickly brand and repurpose. Working together is so much more powerful than working apart. I have seen similar challenges in the corporate world, where the headquarters has one priority, regional offices another, and the brick and mortar individual store, still yet another. If you are already using themes and following a strategic calendar, check to see if everyone in your organization, at all levels, knows what the theme is for the month. It will be a good barometer for the effectiveness of the campaign.

And as you build your risk communications campaigns, do not forget about or give up on self-reliance. Because the next crisis is coming soon.

###

Chapter 3 Crisis Communications

"In a crisis, dont' hide behind anything or anyone. They're going to find you anyway."

- Bear Bryant, former Alabama football coach

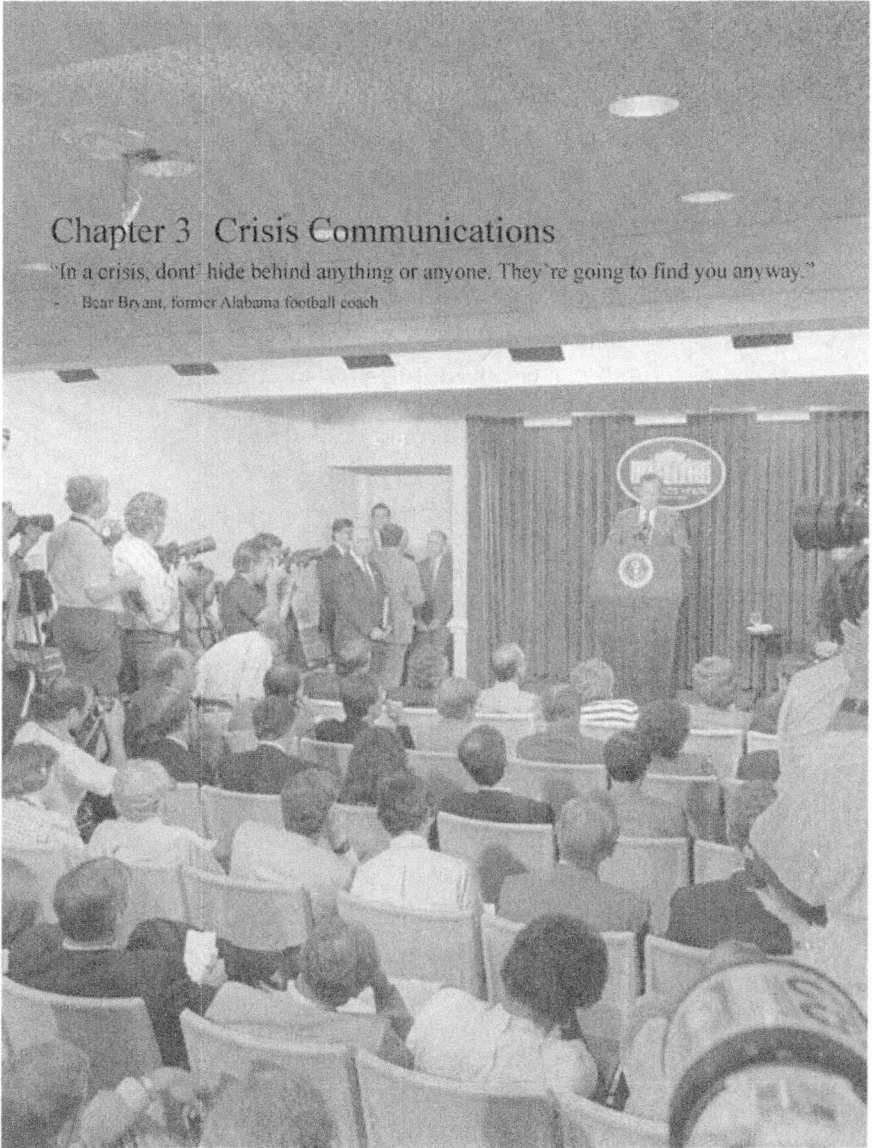

Chapter 3   Crisis Communications by Dan Stoneking

This entire book is about crisis communications, so why does it have a distinct chapter? In addition to the strategic and tactical ideas shared in the rest of the book, I wanted to dedicate some things they might not have told you in formal training and/or you have not yet experienced in a crisis. And it begins by understanding that everyone is in a crisis, including you.

If you have ever taken a trip on a commercial flight, you have certainly heard the guidance, "Should the cabin lose pressure, oxygen masks will drop. Please place the mask over your own mouth and nose before assisting others."[22] The logic is simple, yet lifesaving, because if you run out of oxygen yourself, you cannot help anyone else with their oxygen mask.

Likewise, in a crisis we have to take care of ourselves and our team before we can adequately take care of survivors.

Does that happen in your organization? In my experience, emergency managers not only see every disaster as all hands-on deck, but also any remote possibility of a disaster as all hands-on deck. A+ for readiness, but D- for health,

---

[22] *Make Sure That Your Mask Is On First*, Military.Com

welfare, recruiting and retention. Burn out leads to people seeking employment elsewhere. And who are among the first to leave? Those with the talent, skills, and resumes to quickly be hired elsewhere. So, we lose many of our best. I have heard it and seen it at the local, state, and federal level.

First, let us address the transition from steady state to crisis mode. We have heard these terms so often before, "lean forward," "Go big and go early." Citizens hear similar warnings, "It only takes one hurricane," "You can drown in one inch of water," and "This could be the big one."

But what happens when it is not "the big one" and yet we "lean forward" anyway? Citizens and emergency responders suffer from "crying wolf" and get both jaded and burned-out. I am not suggesting that we disregard being ready. I am simply advocating for a sensible and balanced posture. Nutritionists advocate a balanced diet. Photographers balance their imagery. I balance my bicycle every day I ride. The circus has a balancing act. Even other professions advocate a work-life balance.

And I do not buy that this is necessary due to the mission. I have been both a soldier and an emergency manager. It was easier being a soldier. Even at war, soldiers get rest and rotation because it is the smart thing, the right thing to do. Soldiers have training cycles when they train. So, they would never need to jump into an operation center every time a hurricane is five days away.

I have only retired from full-time work for a short time, and I have already become more productive with less work. When I am tired, I stop. When I get writer's block, I step away and play a game on my phone. Studies have even shown that taking a nap at midday can improve performance. Yet can you imagine an emergency management supervisor walking by your desk while you are snoring or playing another game of Angry Bird on your phone? They love their mantra so much, they will remind you, with a bit of a grunt and a smirk, that this business is not for everyone. I call bull on that.

When you are a supervisor, you can be the difference-maker. I was the lead federal spokesperson in Puerto Rico for the first 30 days after Hurricane Maria hit. On the third day, one of my team was experiencing heart pain. I personally escorted her to the medical area and waited with her until a friend arrived. I was gone for an hour and trusted my team to do the right things in my absence. In that same week, under-staffed, I was chastised by headquarters leadership for not personally being on seven different calls each day. I had staff on those calls and my priority was leading and caring for the team and providing assistance to survivors. After we got through the toughest first week, I gathered the media team together every evening at 7:00 p.m. for a quick huddle to compare notes, sum up the day, and plan for the next. And then I kicked them out and made them go home to get some sleep, and for some of them who were survivors themselves, to spend time with their family. Their motivation was higher and their performance stronger than many of the folks whom I knew stayed much later into the evening, burning themselves out, and reducing productivity.

We can all be responsive, prepared, and effective emergency responders, but not if we fail to put the oxygen mask on ourselves and our teams first.

30,000 Feet

In Chapter 26, I close out the book with four disaster stories I wrote about specific disasters where I was deployed. They may provide you with a more raw and personal understanding about crisis communications, to include some lessons learned. In this chapter, I just want to expand on a few strategic and tactical considerations otherwise not covered. In the previous chapter, I outlined the communication model: The sender → crafts a message → that is filtered by his/her → experiences and environment → the it goes through all kinds of noise and interference, depending on the medium → then through the receiver's environment and experiences → finally to be decrypted into what they receive and hear.

In a crisis it is the same model, except now it is on steroids, flooded with urgency, fear, and misinformation. So, if we are writing at a seventh to eighth grade level in steady state, it is time to dial it down to a fourth to fifth grade level.

Every disaster is different, trite but true. But every crisis has common characteristics as well. In a crisis, you will experience abundantly *more* media queries than normal, while at the same time you experience an information vacuum with *less* content than normal to report. But you will always know some things. Compassion. Empathy. Focus on lifesaving and life-sustaining priorities. Remember that while you are working to get more details on the crisis and how your organization is responding, the media and the community are on information overload. In the first few hours, you do not need to cite a dozen different pieces of information. You do want to address fear and instill confidence in the audience's belief and trust in your organization's ability to respond.

Fortunately, a crisis is not a spectator sport. Invariably you will not be alone in what caused the crisis and certainly will not be alone in responding to the crisis. Former Florida Emergency Manager and Former FEMA Administrator, Craig Fugate, has often explained his 'whole of community' concept.[23] If a neighborhood floods, local, state, and sometimes federal officials will become part of the response. But much more than that, individuals, neighbors, faith-based, non-profits, corporations and more can, and should be, part of the response. Recognizing and repeating this can be both humbling and empowering. Even the media can be part of the solution to educate and inform accurately on crisis response, resources and individual survivor benefits. When you find you are not alone, the questions and the answers both get easier.

Even in a corporate crisis, the company does not always have to face the crisis alone. In 1982, seven people died after taking extra-strength Tylenol capsules that had been laced with potassium cyanide. The parent company, Johnson & Johnson, quickly pulled thirty-one million

---

[23] *Whole of Community*, FEMA

bottles of Tylenol -- $100 million worth -- off the shelves and stopped all production and advertising of the product. It also got involved with the Chicago Police, FBI, and FDA in the search for the killer, and offered up a $100,000 reward.[24] Suddenly and subtly Johnson & Johnson shifted away from the sole position of culpability to one of partnering solutions with other organizations. These relationships can be public to public, private to private, as well as public and private partnerships.

Three Feet

Each crisis is a tragic event. Ironically, they are much easier to message than day to day announcements. If you read enough on this topic, most pundits will give you three key messages. And they seldom go into detail as if they were self-explanatory. I prefer four and prefer adding context will help:

1. **Here is What we Know**: This should be based on fact, well within the lanes of the speaking organization and useful, actionable information for the audiences.
2. **Here is What we are Doing:** The focus here is "progress." If you brief out daily and keep saying the same thing, it will

[24] *9 PR Fiascos That Were Handled Brilliantly By Management*, Insider

sound like you are stagnant. Brief the essential activities the organization accomplished since the last update.

3. **Here is What we Need You to Do:** This should be focused on lifesaving, life-sustaining, and property protection. Connected to that are reminders to avoid certain threats, to stay out of the way of first responders, and encouragement to help a neighbor in need.

4. **Here is What we are Doing Next:** Be careful not to speculate here but demonstrate that you have a plan of action. This will foreshadow what you brief the next day.

I was physically present in the Department of Defense Pentagon Media Briefing Room on February 12, 2002, when Secretary of Defense Donald Rumsfeld made the following statement:

> *"As we know, there are known knowns; there are things we know we know. We also know there are known unknowns; that is to say we know there are some things we do not know. But there are also unknown unknowns—the ones we don't know we don't know."*[25]

---

[25] *Rumsfeld's Knowns and Unknowns,* The Atlantic

On a separate occasion he once referred to an answer he could try to give as 'unbumperstickerable.'" A few weeks after his speech, I actually saw the quote above on a bumper sticker. I share all that to point out that while there are in fact only four things that need to be addressed in a crisis, they each carry essential nuances for the crisis communicator. In the initial stages of a crisis, what the operational subject matter experts know, what the senior leadership knows, and what the spokesperson knows are often not the same. But what each of them knows is far more than the audience knows. Tell them what you do know, the known knowns.
.

Remember Compassion, Conviction, Optimism (CCO) from the previous chapter. You know that. Express it.

I could write and advise all day from the perspective of a seasoned crisis communicator. Sometimes, it is helpful to sneak behind the curtain and learn from victims, survivors, and impacted citizens. In the Summer of 2023, I was one of thousands of community members impacted by the terror of a brutal murderer escaping from a county prison a mere six miles from my home.[26]   So, I will take a moment to share a true story, to provide perspective on crisis communications from the other side.

I cannot imagine the fear among those within the direct radius of the escape and where Law Enforcement Officers (LEO) established perimeters at that time. But, as a father of two young daughters, six miles was close enough for me to triple check the locks often and to not allow my daughters out of the house without me. So, I became an impacted and concerned citizen.

Before I go on, this evaluation is not meant to criticize LEOs nor their Public Information Officers (PIOs). I was on the other side this time and did not have first-hand knowledge of the decisions, experience, or resources to tell their story. But I am sharing my perception. And perceptions become reality, at least my reality. I also will not take time to describe all the details of the escape or the convict. There is enough information in this piece and the footnote for you to learn much more, if you would like, but that is not the purpose here. The purpose here is to simply share the perception of public storytelling from the perspective of one member of that public.

---

[26] *A Convicted Murderer Escaped from Chester County Prison*, The Philadelphia Inquirer

I do not have cable TV, but I have streaming and a computer, so I did not expect that to be a hindrance. At the beginning (Aug 31), and again, ten days into the ongoing escape, I searched the following, with these results.

Pocopson Township Website (where prison is located) – Nothing posted.
Kennett Square Website (nearby town) – Nothing posted, but there were two articles about their Mushroom Festival, which went on as planned, with thousands of people in attendance.
West Chester Police Website – Nothing posted. Last news release was dated June 23
Chester County Website (The search grid for the first ten days) – Nothing posted.
Chester County Prison (from where the convict escaped) – Nothing posted.
Chester County Sheriff Website – Nothing posted.
PA State Police Website – Nothing posted.
PA State Police Facebook Site[27] – To their credit, they posted more information than all the other sources I could find combined. This is the timeline of their posts:

> **Sept 2** First post, informing the public of the escape on Aug 31st

---

[27] PA State Police Facebook Page

Sept 5 An update, including photos of the escaped convict captured on a trail-cam on the property of Longwood Gardens.
Sept 7 9:26 a.m. A Press Briefing with several officials, though there was no advance advisory that it was going to be aired then.
Sept 7 2:59 p.m. Another Press Briefing. Again, no advance advisory.
Sept 9 An update that there had been two confirmed sightings, still in the proximity of Longwood Gardens
Sept 10 An update to share that the escapee had been seen in a *"white 2020 Ford Transit van... in the northern Chester County area near Phoenixville. He changed his appearance. He is now clean shaven and was wearing a yellow or green hooded sweatshirt, black baseball style hat, green prison pants, and white shoes."*

In those first few days I scoured websites, YouTube, Facebook, and NextDoor social media platforms. Each day, I learned more from my social media neighbors than I did from officials. Unfortunately, their information was not always vetted. Many claimed that the convict was long gone, when there was straightforward evidence that he was still in the local area. It is hard as a

PIO to effectively message when there is no interest in the topic. But this was a softball. People were desperate for information. On Sept 8, a PA Trooper PIO posted a very brief update on the *All Things West Chester* Facebook site. I was excited to see him come to where the people were engaging. I posted a thank you with a request to keep posting at a regular drumbeat, but never saw a post from him again.

As an impacted citizen, from the other side, here are my thoughts and observations for the next LEO PIO in a crisis:

- From day one establish a daily drumbeat of Press Briefings, at the same time each day.
- Promote those through every medium possible, well in advance, with advisories.
- Push those advisories to the media, relevant social media platforms, and every local government website that has a role.
- Monitor both mainstream and social media for misinformation and either correct on the spot and/or establish a rumor control section on the LEO website(s) to correct the record.
- Stop the constant barrage of using the convict's name. It unnecessarily humanizes the murderer.

- Use current pictures exclusively. We often saw a photo in an orange jumpsuit where he had much shorter hair than the day he escaped and looked substantively different. Since they had the current photo, it should have been used exclusively.
- Provide a reasonable balance between operational security and providing enough information to inspire confidence and calm fears. It is more than fine to explain that many actions are being taken that are both seen and unseen, but we can share….
- Again, in any crisis, it helps to tell the community: what you have done, what you are doing, what the community needs to do, and what you are going to do next. In this case, we barely got a portion of what they were doing, and not even that daily.
- Hundreds of comments were posted on multiple social media about the Mushroom Festival that attracts thousands every year and whether it should be canceled or not. It was not canceled. I looked to find an LEO position or recommendation on this and found none. People want, and have a right to expect,

fair counsel from their local officials on
their safety.

- In addition to LEOs, the communities
  need to hear from their elected officials. I
  could not find any comments from any
  town official, mayor, or county official.
  There was also nothing on the State
  Governor's website.

As of Sept 11, we did not know how the convict
was able to steal a vehicle and escape from the
established perimeter near Longwood Gardens
and drive twenty-six miles to the Phoenixville
area. That drive passed within a mile of my
home. As a Dad, I was relieved that there was
more distance between the murderer and our
home.

On Sep 13, the convict was caught. Suddenly, the
PA State Police found ways to communicate.
They immediately posted to Facebook, sent
emails and texts to all of us in the community,
and conducted an immediate press conference.
This demonstrates that they have the skills, but
only elected to use them substantively to share
good news, not lifesaving news. After the
capture, several LEOs took a group picture with
the prisoner. If their goal were to simply show he
was caught, an individual picture of the prisoner
in handcuffs would suffice. The group picture
was more about boasting a trophy and self-

congratulatory. That kind of tactic does not typically enhance an organization's reputation. Humility in victory is a better choice, especially after many errors previously. As a citizen and experienced communicator, I hope that future communities have better information while the threat is still outstanding.

In the last chapter, I mentioned *Ready.Gov* as a useful tool. Since the talking points posted there represent before, during, and after for a few dozen different disasters, it saves the crisis communicator several precious minutes, by copying those for review, edit, and a starting point.[28]

I have worked for different organizations at various levels who all have their own policies, procedures, forms, and checklists for a crisis. In all those positions, I have added my own tool that I have found more helpful and useful than all the rest of those combined. I call it ***Feed the Beast.*** No matter where you work, during a real crisis, internal leadership will be clamoring for answers. More often than not, there is leadership higher than them demanding answers. They can be a *beast* in the middle of your day while you are trying to get things done and help survivors, but you have to keep pausing to let someone else

---

[28] *All Hazards, Before, During, and After,* Ready.Gov

know what you are doing and give them comfort that you are doing it well. So, I do not wait for them to ask. I feed them early every morning.

You may not like hearing this, but effective crisis communications means you need to wake up early. The bigger the disaster, the earlier you need to get up. In most of the crises I have worked, 5:00 a.m. is sufficient. I have my news clips person start even earlier unless there is a night shift to cover. You can do this in a thousand different formats and apply nuances to your organization. But before I go to bed the night before, I begin to draft a product, and I complete it when I wake up. I email a document to all the leadership, and cc other relevant internal parties, which include the following:

> 1. Brief executive summary on the communication status
> 2. Three to five key messages for the day
> 3. Products that will be pushed that day
> 4. Outreach schedule for the day (interviews, congressional, town halls, VIP Tours, et al)
> 5. I attach the latest Talking Points, Communication Strategy, and the News Clips

The hardest part of all of that is just waking up. You do the work anyway. Even if there is a process to have one or more of these due at 10:00 am, why wait? This empowers the leadership, builds confidence, and significantly reduces disruptions during the day. Feed the Beast.

I will conclude this chapter with an opinion that may surprise you. I have often been asked what the most important document I review each day in a crisis. Most people will guess talking points or news releases, social media or imagery. Nope. The most important document to me is the Communications Team Personnel Roster. Even if you are a one-person shop, if there is a crisis, there are usually other crisis communicators that have an interest and a role. Checking daily to make sure you have the latest names, roles, phone, and email is essential. You can task out the duty, but you need to review. If you have a team, are their days off scheduled? Does the roster account for arrival and departures? Does it show where people are geographically? If you make sure in every crisis that you have the right people where they need to be and you can reach out to them within seconds, then you are set up for success. This is not sexy or fun, but it is essential. It might be the most crucial tool you have, Well, except for the Strategic Communications Calendar.

###

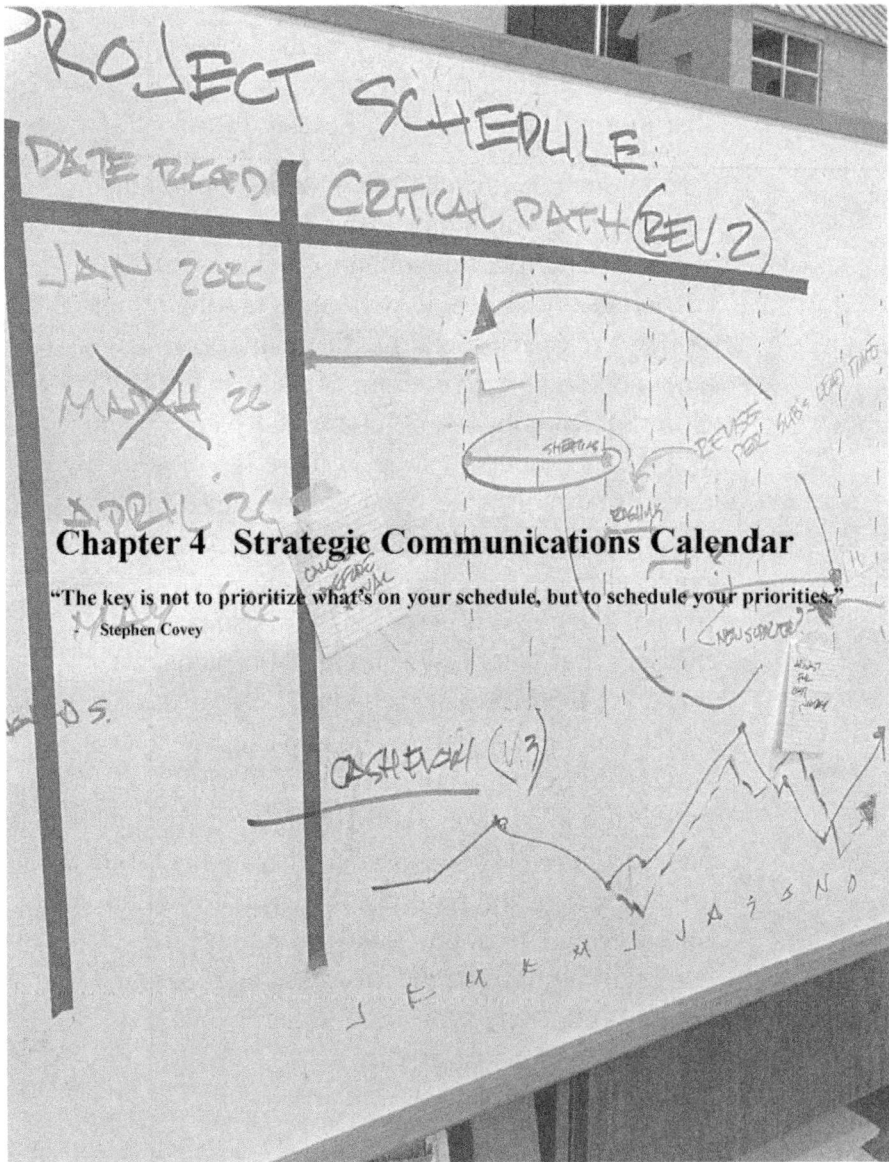

Chapter 4   Strategic Communications Calendar

"The key is not to prioritize what's on your schedule, but to schedule your priorities."
— Stephen Covey

Chapter 4   Strategic Communications
Calendar by Dan Stoneking

I am willing to bet that you have never read a book on crisis communications that has a chapter dedicated to this, the Strategic Communications Calendar. It is true and fair that you have to put the horse before the cart and build the Communications Strategy first. I am not suggesting that you reverse that order. I do, however, advise that when all is said and done, the calendar becomes more important, visible, fluid, and a guide to short and long-term engagements.

Still, I will pause briefly to address the Communication Strategy. You can search for dozens of different versions online and they all have pros and cons. In the end, you pick the one that best suits you and your organization in a meaningful way. I am a fan of simplicity and only writing plans that matter. I endorse a framework, ***organized by program divisions,*** based on four key components:

Goals – What the priorities are for engagement;

Objectives – What are the steps for achieving success;

Tactics – How do we get there; and

Assessments – What does success look like?

Assume your organization has four divisions, Sales, Marketing, Finance, and Operations. In this scenario, you would have a separate section of Goals, Objectives, Tactics, and Assessments for each. This is where many strategies miss the mark and only develop for the whole organization. A tactic that works for sales would not work for operations. Transitioning to an emergency management example, an assessment for response would be quite dissimilar to an assessment for recovery. Finally, to be successful, the development of the strategy must be collaborative between the programs and the communicators. The former know the content, the latter know the outreach.

The strategy is the foundation, but they often fail because after they get published, everyone pats themselves on the back, and then they are filed away and forgotten, at least for the most part. There is no catalyst on a quiet Thursday morning for either the communicator or their divisional counterpart to stop and think, gee, are we employing our communication strategy tactics for the search and rescue team today? This is where the calendar comes in and becomes so vital.

30,000 Feet

A successful Strategic Communications Calendar will capture each of the tactics included in the Communications Strategy, as well as other key events, messaging themes, toolkits, campaigns, ad-hoc storytelling opportunities, anniversaries, and more. The calendar guides outreach efforts and supports the overall execution of the Communications Strategy. To ensure the organization is staying on track to complete the tactics identified in the Communications Strategy, the calendar must be briefed on a regular, ideally biweekly, basis during leadership meetings with all divisions present. Part of that brief should be a review of the previous two weeks and the other part should tee up the two weeks ahead. In addition, the calendar needs to be posted electronically to a share drive or other sharing portal so that updates and edits can be submitted for review and approval, as well as to provide the entire organization a transparent reminder and report card on outreach efforts. In a crisis environment, in addition to the electronic copy, it is helpful to also print out a large poster size week-at-a-glance version with the largest plotter available, so everyone in the organization can see the ongoing activities without having to even pause to search for them.

As much as possible, the content will follow the strategy model. For example, in a disaster recovery situation:

Goal – Local television coverage of recovery efforts

Objective – Media availability at the Disaster Recovery Center on Elm St, Sep 4th

Tactic – Deploy additional public affairs staff, run-through on Sep 3, draft media packets

Assessment – How many stations covered, was the tone positive, did survivor attendance increase

The example above is an incomplete snippet, Clearly not all of that language can be in the calendar. But the tactics can be, and that is enough to lead the biweekly meeting discussions to prepare for and assess the rest.

The first question I would ask when I get to a new organization is - can I see the Strategic Communications Calendar.

Three Feet

When I first got to my last organization, we did not have one. A few years later it became a centerpiece for meetings and decision-making. If your organization does not have one, the question becomes how you design one. Like the strategy, it is easy to search online and find a format that works well for your situation. Our calendar had double what you see below, but many of them were only necessary for the communicators. The following columns, however, are basic and essential.

Let us break this sample down. One of the first things you notice is that not every block has an action every day. That can be overwhelming and is often not essential or applicable. For example, On Sep 4, a press release on the amount of funds being obligated for recovery is worthy of a news release, but there is typically not a photo that would accompany that. The Sep 5 row demonstrates that it is important to include preparation activities. Again, this helps both communicators and operators to know that an advisory is going out and the dry run needs active participation. Note then when a collaborative activity is occurring, like the media availability on Sep 6, the POC should include contact information for the POC. Invariably, someone will need to reach out to that person quickly on that day. I added Sep 7 to highlight two important actions after an event. The communicators need to do a deeper than usual dive on the news clips to identify what coverage came out of the event. The bigger the event, the more hullabaloo you should do in media monitoring. Communicators need to remember the importance of sharing successes with the leadership team as a constant reminder of our value. Also, every major event needs to be followed by a lessons-learned, after-action, or hotwash type of discussion. It does not have to be the very next day, but it should be done as soon as possible and include all of the participants. Otherwise, some planner will write up a report that may or may not capture events accurately.

Date	Theme	Story	Activity	Photos
Sep 4	Recovery	$$	Release	n/a
Sep 5	Recovery	Center	Advisory Dry- Run	
Sep 6	Recovery	Center	Media Availability	Deploy Jones
Sep 7	Recovery	Center	Review News Clips Conduct Hotwash	n/a

Videos	Location	POC	Media	Social Media
n/a	n/a	Smith	Full Distro	Tweet
	n/a Elm St	Davis	TV Distro	Instagram
Share B-Roll	Elm St	Johnson Email Phone	By RSVP	FB Live
n/a	Conference Room	Miller	n/a	n/a

So, that is the content. A few words on the process. An effective calendar will include a mechanism where anyone can suggest an edit, addition, or deletion. But those must always be reviewed before they are applied by a member of the communications team. There has to be a gatekeeper to eliminate redundancies and ensure accuracy. During the bi-weekly meetings when the calendar is reviewed, it works best to have the calendar on the conference room screens for all to view. Ideally it will be linked to one of your colleague's laptops, so if the leadership team decides to change an upcoming activity, everyone can see that it is handled immediately.

Management of your calendar is best assigned to a member of the team who excels in attention to detail and being responsive. The entire organization will have eyes on this.

###

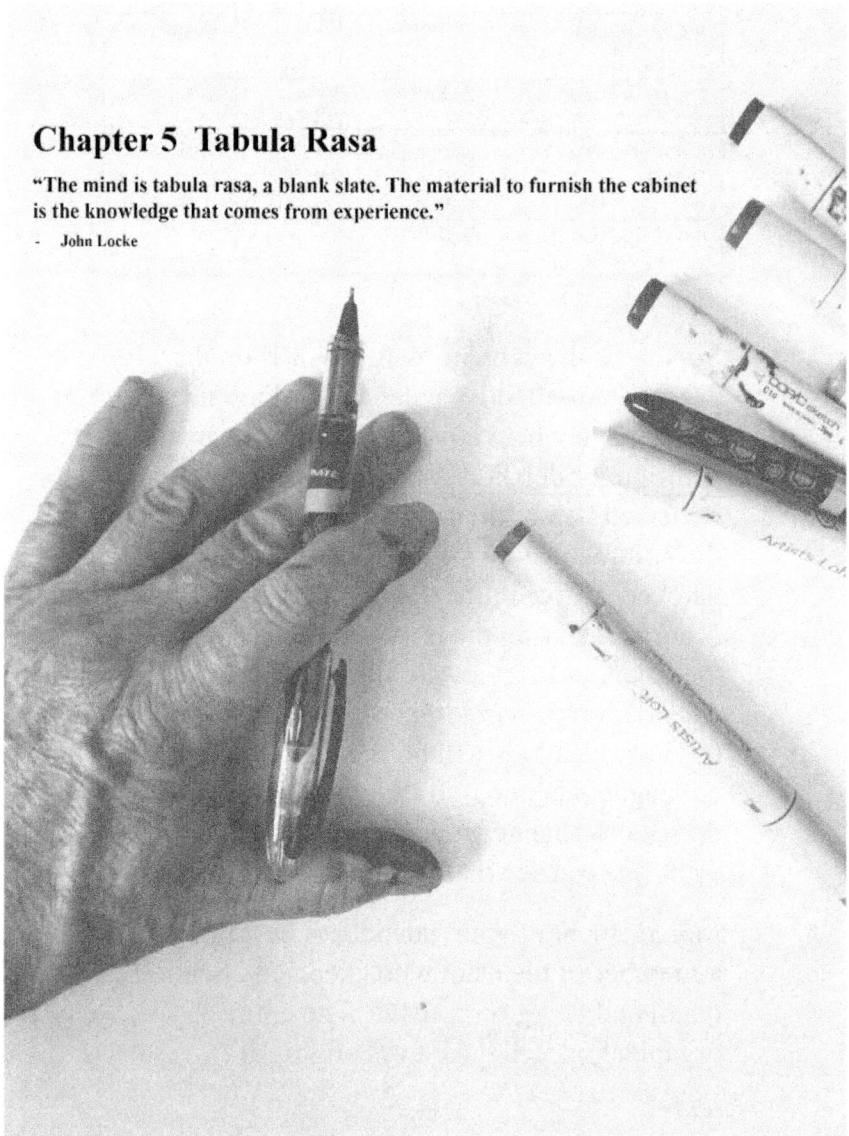

Chapter 5 Tabula Rasa

"The mind is tabula rasa, a blank slate. The material to furnish the cabinet is the knowledge that comes from experience."

- John Locke

Chapter 5   Tabula Rasa by Dan Stoneking

I stole an idea from an architect.

Neuroplasticity is a big word. I looked it up.
When I did, I just came upon more big words like
neuron pathways and cortical remapping. But
after a little digging and reading it twice, I think
the main gist of it is that we can reorganize and
rewire our brains to an extent. Children are better
at this (like most things). It can help after a brain
injury too. I came across this word while surfing
social media. The guy who referenced it said that
if you are right-handed, you should switch
brushing your teeth to your left hand. He also
said to take twenty-five deep breaths three times
a day. He said it would change your life. That is
what got me. I tried the deep breaths and got
bored after seven. So, I went to the bathroom and
brushed my teeth left-handed. It was even more
awkward than I anticipated. I kept looking at my
right hand thinking, you are not helping at all. I
am going to see if I can keep it going. I am all
about growth. But that is not the thing I stole.

As I thought more about it, I made a mental
connection (wow, working already). My brother
Mike is an architect. He shared with me his
slogan and ethos for his work – *Draw What You
Mean*. He explained that if you draw to meet the
needs of the construction crew, it will be an easy

build but not very innovative. If you draw to meet a budget, you limit potential that may arouse the client. And, if you draw to meet the expectations of the client, you have entrusted your craft to someone with zero experience and any appreciation for what is possible. That is worse than lawyers defending themselves and doctors performing surgery on themselves. At least they know the profession.

So, Mike told me that he always starts with drawing what he means.[29] His profession. His art. His vision. He spent years learning and perfecting his craft. He draws what he means to derive the optimum solution. He understands the construction challenges. He can follow a budget. And he certainly listens to the client. But the starting point to draw what he means is a personal commitment and duty to stay true to oneself. It is about setting a priority to the internal process. After his hand sketch is done, the other steps still remain. He will run it through CAD and Revit 3D modeling. He submits a presentation to the client. To be fair, things will change. The client is the customer. Some resources might not be available for the job. Still, when the next project comes, he will once again start by drawing what he means in his faded

---

[29] Stoneking von Storch Architects

Moleskine sketchbook. The way that he has reorganized and rewired this process, much like neuroplasticity, results in more creative and innovative designs, as well as happier clients. It made perfect sense. So, I stole the idea.

30,000 Feet

I stole the idea and applied it to crisis communications. If we write for leadership, we risk unnecessary grip-and-grins, and typically bureaucratic language. If we write for the media, we will end up with sensationalistic results and a damaged reputation. If we write for what we think the general public wants to hear, we risk losing focus among multiple audiences based on our instincts alone. We also lose our personal vision and perspective in our craft. So, I have adopted the *Draw What You Mean* ethos.

While serving in a crisis communications role not too long ago, I was given a draft of a news release that tried to explain the value of buying out homes and demolishing them in a flood zone. It was written primarily by subject matter experts. Too often in our field, communicators go to experts and take what they are given without editing. They are experts in what they do; we are experts in how to convey that. It was complicated and convoluted. I tried to make edits, but no matter what I tried, I knew the average person would not understand it. Instead, I started from nothing, and I asked the reader to picture a football field with fifteen houses on it and flood waters racing in and getting higher because all the buildings created obstacles for run-off. Then I asked them to picture that same football field with only five houses on it and imagine how swiftly the water could spread out and run off, creating less, if any damage. Finally, I let them know that the families who agreed to the demolition did so voluntarily and with fair compensation to build in a safer place. Win, Win, Win. And more importantly, easier to understand.

I drew what I meant. Like the architect, our work still has to go through review and meet certain standards. AP Style. Lawyers. Subject Matter Experts. But, like Mike, if we commit to a starting and focus point of drawing what we mean, each time, the results can change our lives.

I may never fully understand the concept of neuroplasticity. I have never been an architect. But I do know that we can reorganize the way we write, tell human stories that are relatable, and rewire our craft to make a more meaningful difference.

Now, if I can only learn how to brush my teeth left-handed.

Three Feet

Gather the team around. Either share an old release or raise a new topic. Tell your team to forget everything they were ever taught. Give them a day and challenge them to tell the story the way they would want to tell the story. Get back together and discuss and brainstorm novel approaches based on what folks bring to the table.

I know it is hard to break the status quo, so the next time you need to publish something, you can offer your boss one version that is standard and another that stems from your own blank slate. No risk. Potential great upside.

The blank slate can be applied to much more than writing. Take a look around. If you were going to create your environment from nothing, would it look the same way? I am a big believer in the concept of "if it ain't broke, don't fix it." In addition, it would be sloppy to change too many things at once. But over time, take a hard look at all aspects of the job, brainstorm with the team if you have one, and at least challenge the notion of "that's the way we've always done it."

Start with seating. I have worked in offices with doors and cubicles with six foot partitions. I also worked in the Pentagon where it was open seating for about twenty of us in a shared area. I preferred the latter as it naturally created more collaboration. But what works for you? Is the team lead with the staff or apart? Is the senior communicator close to the boss or far away? Do the seats adapt to people who prefer to stand while they work? Are there any plants? I am not advising here on what or how to do seating. I am simply conveying that the choices should be strategic and stem from your vision and not just what you inherit.

Duty hours are another opportunity to draw it the way you see it on your blank slate. There are different rules and variances between the public and private sector, but there is always room to reassess. When you review individual and team hours, would you have drawn it that way? My preference is to give people as much flexibility within the established formal rules. I understand that not everyone is comfortable with that. Teams work better with some early risers and some who are later. That ensures more representation and coverage. If news clips are a responsibility, it works well to have someone start early enough to complete them before senior leadership turn on their computers.   Is teleworking or remote work an option? Has every option been considered? Did the staff get a voice in the final decisions?

Some of you, more so in the corporate world, may have complete control over this, so I will share a quick story. Many years ago, I was being assigned a role as a training officer with only two people whom I would supervise. Before the first day, I was told that these two individuals were lazy, unproductive, and difficult. They were mine to 'fix" and I had all the latitude I needed to do so. I met them Monday morning at 8:00 a.m. and I shared a lengthy list of things I wanted accomplished that week. I told them if they were not completed by Friday, we would be working the weekend. But on the other hand, if they were to finish anytime earlier in the week, they could have the rest of the week off. They approached me on that Wednesday at 10:00 a.m. to show me all the work completed. It was clean, professional, and meticulous. As I approved the work they laughed and reminded me that I had to let them have the rest of the week off. I smiled as I confirmed that they indeed could have the rest of the week off and that I look forward to seeing them Monday and now that I know what they can complete in 20 hours, we can raise the bar! It should never be about the hours, but rather about getting the work done.

If you are leading a team, would you have created all of the roles that currently exist, and would you have assigned them to the people who have them now? Even if you do not have the power, or think you do not have the power, sit down and draw the organization chart with the roles and assignments the way you would have drawn it. Even if it is a small thing like assigning quality control, or internal communications lead, you can still effect change, drawing what you mean.

There are countless opportunities to start with a blank slate mentality, but I will offer one more - websites. As I type this and imagine myriad people reading these words, I anticipate that a large majority of you, unless you are the webmaster, do not particularly love your organization's website. What would you change? In my blank slate, I want my website to serve citizens and survivors, but also stakeholders with whom we collaborate. I would want it to be visually compelling, up to date, and intuitive to navigate. What would yours look like?

In closing, I know this can all feel overwhelming and difficult to accomplish. But do not look at it that way. These are opportunities. And small victories can make a massive difference. Again, just like the architect, you will need to bend, compromise, and abide at times. But at least you are starting with true, strong, and righteous intent.

###

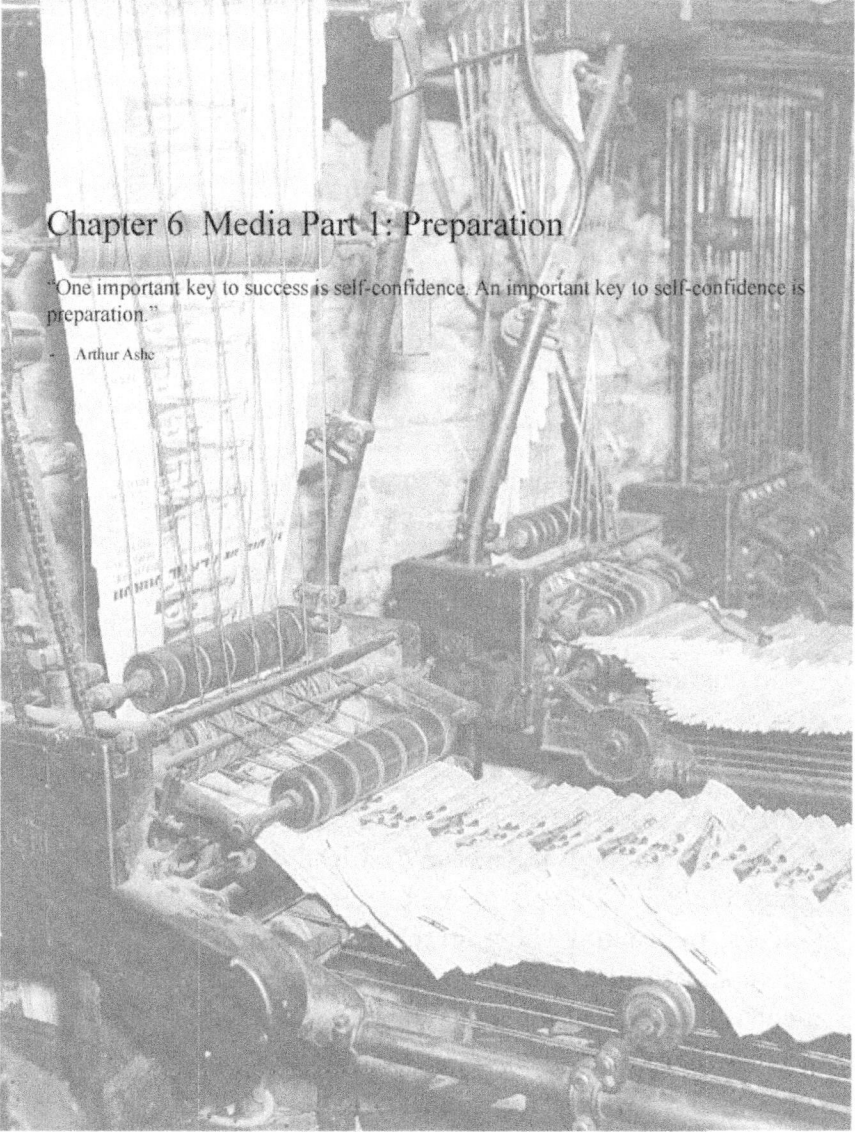

Chapter 6 Media Part 1: Preparation

"One important key to success is self-confidence. An important key to self-confidence is preparation."

- Arthur Ashe

Chapter 6   Media Part 1: Preparation by Dan
Stoneking

Have you ever heard the fable of "The Wild
Boar and the Fox?"[30] It goes like this:

*"The Fox asks the Wild Boar why he is
sharpening his tusks when there is no danger in
sight. The Wild Boar points out that when the
danger does arrive, he will not have time to
sharpen his weapons. Moral: Preparedness for
war is the best guarantee of peace."*

This is such a great analogy for preparing for
media interviews. Because if the communicators
do not sharpen their tusks, the media may
sharpen their tusks, and then beware when the
boss sharpens her tusks. As the moral goes, you
can guarantee peace with simple preparedness.

The worst interview I have ever seen occurred in
January 2014, four days after chemical company
Freedom Industries was responsible for a spillage
that polluted the Elk River in Charleston, WV,
impacting 300,000 people who were left without
access to drinking water. In that interview, the
company president appeared rude, aloof,
complained about it being a long day for him,
and actually had the audacity to drink from a

---

[30] *The Wild boar and the Fox,* The Fables of Aesop

water bottle while thousands were denied the same simple right due to his company's negligence.[31] I often wonder who, if anyone, prepared him for that interview.

30,000 Feet

There are myriad types of leaders. They all have strengths, and they all have weaknesses. Our job is to know who among the leadership team may speak on behalf of the organization, which ones are skilled, and which ones are not. And do you know which ones you need to prepare for each interview? All of them. As part of your strategic plan, schedule any and all potential spokespersons for media training. It is essential that the training includes mock interviews on camera, so you can playback to show strengths and areas of improvement individually to avoid any embarrassment.

Strategically, when pitching to media and considering requests, the first step is to understand the differences and nuances among the mediums

Television interviews are the only ones where body language and appearance are absolutely essential. This is nothing new. On 26 September 1960, Richard Nixon and John F. Kennedy met

---

[31] *"We're Not Done!"* DailyMail.com

for their first debate. It was the first televised presidential debate in history. Nixon was described as sweaty, "he often looked nervous and shifty in cutaway shots, glancing from side to side and curling his lip while Kennedy spoke."[32] Scholars and historians alike have agreed that Nixon's appearance cost him the election. Think of the profound impact of that and the vastly different path our nation may have taken without ever having Kennedy in office. This is nothing new, but many decades later we still witness similar mistakes.

When you can choose who to be a spokesperson for television interviews, pick someone who is quick on their feet. There is no time for dead air. In my experience, many leaders preferred taped interviews. They think they are safer since thousands or millions are not watching them live. They are wrong. Opting for tape lulls speakers into a false sense of security, which leads to more mistakes. In a taped television interview, the reporter has all the power. They may tape ten minutes and only use two minutes. And we do not get to decide which two minutes those are. On the other hand, in a live interview the adrenaline and fear tend to keep the spokesperson on message and on track. And the spokesperson

[32] *"Did Nixon's sweaty, shifty debate performance cost him the presidency?"* Independent

has all the power. It is live. Whatever we say cannot be edited. When it is live, be cognizant of time to ensure all key messages are leveraged. Finally, offer media crawls, banner, b-roll or other video packages (sometimes for picture-in-picture too). They just may use them.

Radio interviews free the spokesperson from most of the nonverbal issues, but that just makes the remaining issue - tone - more important. We will take a deeper dive on this in a later issue, but you can solve most challenges in prep sessions by identifying and addressing the speaker's greatest weakness. Do they speak too fast? Do they mumble? I was once preparing two women for a radio spot they were going to share. I had to tell one of them that she used too many big words and sounded like a lawyer. I had to tell the other one that she did not sound compassionate. They both listened and did a brilliant job. Sometimes, less is more. It is also helpful to provide the radio show producer and/or talent with the organizational link and even one key message in advance, as they will often quote these to the audience before and after the interview, giving your talking points more mileage. Brevity and clarity rule the radio airwaves. Do not say in seven sentences what you can say in seven words. Yet, repetition is a good thing to ensure your message is heard.

When my son was about eight years old, I could never get him to clean up his room. I would tell him once and expect it to be done. However, when his kind and patient grandmother would come for visits, she would keep repeating, "Karl, go clean your room. Let's go, Karl. It is time to clean your room. You want your room to be all clean and nice. Karl…" And just at the point where I found it annoying, it clicked for him and off he would go. FEMA Administrator Craig Fugate spoke about the whole community approach to emergency management more than a hundred times before local and state officials, along with the media, began to use the term in their own discourse.[33]

Most radio interviews occur by phone. In those instances, remind the speaker to have all the visual aids at their disposal. If they have two monitors, one can be opened to the organizational web page that supports the topic. Another monitor could have information about the radio station, host, and audience. And more information, like key messages and talking points can be printed in 14 or 16 point font. Just ensure that your speaker has the skills to use these resources without sounding like they are robotically reading verbatim. For some people

---

[33] The Whole Community Approach to Emergency Management

that comes naturally. For others it must be learned and rehearsed.

Print interviews offer a few opportunities unique from the other mediums. Typically, both television and radio will go by the audience quickly, while a newspaper can be read and re-read at the reader's pace. It offers opportunities for more detail, explanation, and background. Provide the reporter with all the fact sheets, releases, and links that can help them tell the story more fully and accurately. Also, offer images. With rising costs and smaller staffs and budgets, most reporters no longer bring a photographer. In fact, it is increasingly rare that the reporter will visit, conducting the interview by phone instead. I have seldom been asked by a print reporter for photographs, yet when I offer them, I have experienced a high rate of acceptance. I even provide captions. Sometimes they use them, sometimes they edit them. But there is always a chance to further shape the story. Print is a great vehicle for statistics as well. The reader has the time to soak in the details and the impact. Speaking of time, since print is not live, you can always contact the reporter after an interview to provide a point or a quote that you feel was missed in the interview. Lastly, while it is a prudent idea for us to always record any interview ourselves, it is even more essential with print. Your recording might be the only evidence you have if there is a dispute over the accuracy of the article.

The internet is the past, present and future. Whenever doing television, radio, or print, we should always determine if the interview will also be included on their web page, which is often the case. Make sure your speaker knows that their words may still be searchable for years to come. Add their internet address to your news clip search list. For live television and radio airing on the internet, make sure they receive your material for media crawls, banners, links, imagery, et al. Be aware that you may need to find a different contact for the media's internet than their original point of contact.

Three Feet

Here is a *passive* example of how I have seen many communicators prepare their boss for an interview:

"Hey boss, The Daily Press wants to interview you about the disaster at 4:00 pm. I put it on your calendar. Let me know if you need talking points." Yikes. Do not be that person.

Instead make a habit, whenever possible, to provide your boss with the following, *active* preparation:

- ***Logistics.*** Who, what, where, why, when, and how. This information should also be in the electronic calendar invitation.
- ***Key Messages.*** These are the things you *want* them to say. If they are face-to-face with the reporter, three key messages should suffice. If the interview is telephoned, you can expand to five. Each of these needs to be clear, tight, impactful, and memorable.
    - "We rescued 52 survivors today."
    - "This hurricane will kill people. Evacuate now."
    - "Today, we donated $5 million to speed up recovery."
- ***Anecdote.*** Provide a true, human interest anecdote or short story that the speaker can use to motivate and inspire audiences. Oftentimes, your leadership during a crisis already has experienced or witnessed these and you just need to draw them out and capture them. Each crisis is a tragic story; every response can be a heroic story. Be a storyteller.
- ***Talking Points.*** These are things you are *happy* to say. They may not be as powerful as the few key messages, but they provide details, context, and will help the speaker address any aspect of the operation. Each individual talking point

should be clear and tight like the key
messages, but you may have many more
of them. In some cases, they can expand
to a few pages. In those cases, break them
down by categories and sub-headings like
Search and Rescue, Response, Power,
Recovery Centers, et al. The headings
will vary by organizations and incidents,
but they will facilitate the speaker's recall
as opposed to scrolling through two pages
of 30 bullets.

- ***Tone and Physiology Points.*** In a future
chapter we will address how nonverbals
are more important than what is said,
however most people fail to address them
during preparation. Remind the boss to
express compassion. Encourage the wear
of tactical branded clothing when
appropriate. If they tend to ruffle papers
at a lectern, remind them not to do that.

- ***Response to Query.*** These are the things
you *do not want to say*, but you may have
to if asked. This is also where most
organizations fail because they do not
address the toughest and worst questions
in the preparation and rehearsal phase.
Better that you prepare the speaker rather
than the tough question gets asked
without a prepared response ready. In
your package, keep this section all in red

font to remind your principal visually to be ready, but avoid it if possible.

- **_Background._** This may include historical context, rosters, charts, and other related data. Evaluate how much to include here based on the likelihood of needing the reference material to respond to questions balanced with the speaker's ability to retain information. This is information that *may be asked* but requires more detail to answer.
- **_Media Information._** Whenever time allows, include information on the requesting media, the host, the reporter. Provide Bios and examples of previously published material.
- **_Mock interview._** When you have time and resources and your speaker is average to weak, do these prior. When time is tight and the speaker is talented, skip them. Just always consider them as part of the preparation and make the strategic decision.

A final consideration when preparing for interviews, which can happen and change at any point in the process, is a recommendation of who should take the interview and whether others should be present. Of course, the communicator should staff the interview. But sometimes having a subject matter expert present would be prudent. Having too many people present makes the organization look defensive. I have been in many organizations where the communicator thrives on talking to the media and the leadership are loath to engage. That should not be a deciding factor at all. During a crisis, if a reporter is seeking statistics or mundane information, the communicator can take that role and free up the leader to focus on urgent operational issues. But when there is a life-saving issue and/or the organization's reputation is on the line, the leader should be front and center.

###

Chapter 7   Media Part 2: Ground Rules

"Chess helps you to concentrate, improve your logic. It teaches you to play by the rules and take responsibility for your actions, how to problem solve in an uncertain environment." - Garry Kasparov

Chapter 7   Media Part 2: Ground Rules by Dan Stoneking

When Boris Spassky was losing to Bobby Fischer during their sixth game in 1972, I wonder if Boris ever wished he could simply jump over one of Bobby's pieces like it was checkers, to change the flow and the outcome. Unfortunately for Boris, Bobby opened the game with an uncharacteristic and strategic first move.[34]   In checkers, there are only seven possible opening moves. In chess, there are twenty opening moves that quickly expand above 1,000 moves. Poor Boris was not playing checkers; he was playing chess, and he lost that game and the next.

Media engagement is chess. It depends on strategy. To be effective, you have to think of several moves ahead. You have to be aware of who you are playing, what they are thinking, and what their next move may be. You have to understand when to sacrifice and when not to do so. You need to know how to protect the King, the difference between a bishop and a knight, and the role of pawns, even if it is just en passant.

Both chess and media engagement are about shaping the environment and shaping the outcome.

---

[34] *"Fischer-Spassky, Game Six,"* Chessbase

30,000 Feet

Through life, we learn many ground rules, often from mom and dad. If it sounds too good to be true, it is. Be kind. We are responsible for our actions. Believe in yourself. Do not believe everything you read. Everything is in moderation. They help to guide and protect us. The rules we follow shape the kinds of people we become. The same is true of media ground rules. It would be sloppy to move that first pawn forward without being an expert on the rules. And apply them. That is where the shaping comes in.

The media in the United States has been referred to as both the "Fourth Estate" and the "Fourth Pillar of Democracy." In that role,

> "The media acts as a watchdog and exposes any corruption, scandal or abuse of power that could harm the public. In this sense, it serves as a mediator between the government and the public by providing crucial information that can influence people's opinions and decisions. Therefore, the media is not only a source of news but also a crucial element in maintaining the health and stability of a democracy."[35]

---

[35] *"The Fourth Estate,"* Fairgaze

While their role is critical to ensure a check and balance, that does not mean they are always objective, unbiased, or accurate. Given that they *influence people's opinions and decisions*, it is equally critical that crisis communicators provide a check and balance in return.

Both parties have the responsibility and ability to shape the story. The devil is in the details.

In the previous chapter we addressed the difference in preparation between a passive and active posture. The same is true when developing ground rules.

Three Feet

This is what _passive_ crisis communications looks like in terms of ground rules:

Reporter: *"Hi, can I get your emergency manager on the phone for a quick chat about this disaster response?"*

Crisis Communicator: *"Sure, let me set that up for you."*

Active crisis communications are composed of two key components, interviewing the reporter and spokesperson rights. Here is what they look like:

Interview the Reporter

When you get that call, remember that you are playing chess. It starts when they move a piece, like a pawn. Your next move does not have to be tipping your king over. They want to interview someone in your organization, so it is only fair that you interview them first. Bring the queenside bishop pawn forward to c5. This begins the classic Sicilian Defense. Consider the next six moves on the board.

- Logistics. Make sure the who, what, when, why, where, and how are clear in the request. If parts are missing, ask them to fill in the blanks. Even if you receive the request through a phone call, you can ask the reporter to follow-up with an email. This gives you more time to process and ensure accuracy.

- Focus/Perspective. Pulse the reporter for the full picture. Their initial request may have been (and often is) general, like asking for an "update on the crisis." Dig deeper. Ask if the interview is part of a bigger story. Are there certain aspects of the disaster that are more pertinent? If you get pushback, you can explain that it is necessary in order for you to offer the appropriate spokesperson(s) to save everyone time. Another good question is to ask what inspired the query. You may find that they are really interested in allegations of fraud. Had you not asked questions, your leadership could have been blind-sided. Yep. It really happens.

- Deadline Negotiable. Communicators tend to err on the side of accepting any deadline given. This too can often be negotiated. Start by figuring out if that is necessary. If the reporter tells you at 9:00 a.m., that their deadline is 2:00 p.m. and they are going to publish with or without a response, then the deadline is hard. But you still have a choice. If there is any chance of controversy or injured reputation, you are better served to find a way to provide some kind of response in time. That could be the interview, or it could simply be a prepared statement or quote. By giving something, anything, the reporter is precluded from claiming you refused to comment and/or did not provide feedback prior to the deadline. On the other hand, if the query is benign and/or you have more impactful media competing for time and opportunity, you can decline either the deadline or the entire request (if it is for an interview) and establish your own priorities.
- Scope. It is always fair game to ask who else they are interviewing. You may be

surprised how often they will tell you. If it is an adversary, you just gained valuable context. If it is an ally, you have an opportunity to align and synchronize messaging. Most reporters do not flat out lie, so if they say nobody, that is useful information too. You can suggest other organizations that would help complete the story. You can shape. If they decline to share that information, then they are interviewing others, and you should do your own research to determine who that may be and the impacts.

- Format. If not already covered in the coordination of the request, it is essential to verify the medium (TV, Radio, Print, Web) as well whether it will be live or taped, if applicable, and when the piece will run (makes the media monitoring easier)
- Alternative Interviewee(s). People are negotiable as well. They usually want to talk to the most senior person. The most senior person is usually pretty busy in a disaster. See if they will accept other key officials if either the boss is too busy or someone else is a more appropriate subject matter expert. If you want to have your boss and a subject matter expert, you do not even need to ask. Just do it.

That seems like a lot, right? I just shared six paragraphs about a conversation. But in reality, I have had those conversations in less than a few minutes. And they go even faster if you tell them the information you need and ask them to email it to you. You can even put these six topics in a template that requestors must fill out. Practice this drill with your media desk or team until it is second nature. And if you read the previous chapter closely, you are going to need all this for the prep package anyway.

Spokesperson Rights

It takes two to play. You both have a role in maintaining the health and stability of a democracy. Your role is no less and is sometimes more. You also are the gatekeeper of the information. This gives you rights and responsibilities. You only had six topics to discuss with the reporter, so let us double that and give you a dozen rights.

- Determine COA. This is your call, not theirs. You can accept, decline, or offer another option. The choice should be strategic, not compliant. Determine the option that will best serve the crisis. You want to demonstrate that your organization is addressing the crisis, and is doing so with integrity, competence, and commitment. You want to earn the trust of the community you serve. Pick the option that does that.

- Determine Interviewee(s). As determined in the questions above, whether they are who the reporter wants, you still have the right to determine who the reporter gets.
- Questions in advance. The reporter may decline, but you can and should ask for written questions in advance. Do not make it come off as they are doing you a favor. You are doing them a favor because questions in advance will ensure that you have the right person(s) with the right information, to ensure a meaningful interview for both parties. At the same time, you will be better prepared with effective key messages.
- Attribution. There are three basic options. On the record. Off the record. On background. When an interview is on the record, everything that is said, may be quoted, printed, aired. Be careful, because that includes any asides and comments at the beginning and end that may seem more informal. Anything off the record can simply not be used. Interviews on background can be a little more confusing since you can negotiate the attribution to varied levels. For example, an interview

could be attributed to a government official, a federal government official, a FEMA official, and so on. Here is how you can manage this simply. Always go on the record. Some people find that counterintuitive, so stay with me. When people go off the record, even when the agreement is enforced, the reporter has added information that they can turn into a new question later on with you or someone else, but next time on the record. Going on background seems like a compromise, but more often than not people can figure out who it is and when they cannot the information is seen as less credible, and the source's integrity is questioned. Many in leadership think that off the record and background is safer. Your job is to educate them on that false sense of security. Going on the record keeps everyone on their toes, clean, professional, and easy. In those instances where you are required to one of the other attributions, still remind your speakers to consider everything they say as being on the record anyway for their own protection.

- Offer to Fact Check. I always make the offer to fact check an article after it is written and before it is published. Some accept. Some do not. No harm in asking. Most reporters want to do a respectable job and care about their reputation too. If the issue is complex or has nuances, let them know. They will be more inclined to take you up on it. If they decline and make an error, you can not only correct the record, but also raise with their editor if it is a pattern of behavior or particularly egregious.

- Duration of Interview. They can ask for an hour, and you can agree to only thirty minutes. The more time you allow, the more time for a mistake, a slip, or a gaffe. I am a fan of short interviews. Get to it. Get done. Respect everyone's time. It is always the communicator's job to interrupt at the appropriate closing minute and allow for one last question. Be the bad cop. Do not make the interviewee end it. Protect their reputation.

- Record the interview. Whenever possible, but especially in print, it is good business to have your own recording of every interview. Certainly, you need to inform the reporter you are doing so, but you do not need their permission. If they do not want to be recorded, I would cancel the interview. And I have never had to do that. In addition to protection, these recordings can be a great tool for future training.

- Offer Focus. You and your colleagues will invariably know more about the topic than the reporter. They may have a misguided focus. They may not have any focus. Confront a problem head-on. Make a compelling human interest argument for the focus you present and then provide all the access and resources to get that story told.

- Provide Context. If content is king on the chessboard, then context is queen. And it is still underrated. Have you ever heard the analogy of three blind men touching an elephant? The one grabbing his tail thinks the elephant is a rope. The one touching the tusks thinks the elephant is a spear. And the one touching his trunk thinks it is a snake. Cute. But lack of context in a crisis can be devastating. A little bit of water does not sound scary, even when there is mild flooding in your neighborhood. But when you learn that one can drown in 1.5 inches of water, that six inches of water can make an adult fall, and a foot of water can make most vehicles float, then we have a hugely different perception of that water. And here is the thing about your organization during a crisis - everything has context. Often the reporter will not ask or even know to ask. You have the right and responsibility to fill it.

- Media Monitoring. Of course, most organizations know they have this right and employ some version of tracking and news clips. Most can expand on this. For every interview or query you can ask when and where the story will be published and add that to your search. But do not forget to retroactively monitor the media. When you get a request, go back and look at what that reporter and media have said before.
- Correct Mistakes. We all make mistakes. When reporters make them, you have the right to correct the record and even ask for a retraction. But be strategic in your decision. If the story does not have any legs (continued interest) it may not be worth the time and effort. When you do correct, correct errors in fact. Do not debate opinions. As the saying goes, "never argue with anyone who buys ink by the barrel." In other words, it is not useful to get in a fight with the media.
- Ground Rules in Writing. Lastly, it is your right and responsibility to ask the reporter to agree to all the established

ground rules in writing. Email will suffice.

Ground rules do not ensure that you will win every time. Sometimes you lose. Sometimes it is a stalemate. And sometimes in a crisis you will be moving so fast and be so busy that you cannot complete all six steps in interviewing the reporter and protect yourself with all twelve rights. But if you even add a step or two and a right or two more than you did yesterday, you will reap the rewards.

###

Chapter 8 Media Part 3: Questions

"Questions are never indiscreet, answers sometimes are."
- Oscar Wilde

"Sometimes the questions are complicated and the answers are simple."
-Dr. Seuss

Chapter 8   Media Part 3: Questions by Dan Stoneking

Questions are fascinating. I can still remember my third grade teacher, Miss Earle, teaching us the four types of sentences, the declarative, the imperative, the exclamatory, and the interrogative. I guess I should have been excited about the exclamatory, but I was in awe of the interrogative. It started simple enough. I suppose there should have been more to it, but when we had to identify different examples, I just looked for the question mark. I loved how easy that type of sentence was. More than that, at that age, I was immersed in so many questions of my own. Are we alone in the universe? Why do we dream? Do ghosts exist? What makes peanut butter and jelly taste so good? I felt like I had all the power and none of the responsibility.

Then one day, all of a sudden, I was grown-up, a spokesperson, and other people got to ask the questions and I had to produce answers. Even more difficult than that, I had to learn how to coach and prepare other people on how to answer questions. I am still fascinated with questions. They just are not as easy as they were in third grade.

If you have worked in crisis communications for more than a day, then you have written talking points. You have the declaratives mastered. That is an entry level skill. Interrogatives are more nuanced and can be manipulated. How they are managed can make the difference between success and failure in a crisis. So, they are worth a chapter.

30,000 Feet

If I were to tell you right now that I know that when the next crisis occurs, I know the first few questions you will get, would that help? I am happy to oblige. You will be asked some version of the following:

1. What happened?
2. What are you doing about it?
3. What should the people being impacted by this crisis be doing?
4. What are you going to do next?

That is precisely why, in Chapter 3, we primed you with your first key messages:

1. Here is what we know.
2. Here is what we are doing.
3. Here is what we need you to do.
4. Here is what we are doing next.

So, do not wait for these questions. That puts you on the defensive. Lead with these messages. Push out a news release. Saturate social media. Host a press conference. And when/if you are interviewed, shape the environment by including these in your opening statement.

Questions 5 through 10 will vary with the crisis. *Anticipate* them. If there is a power outage, you will be asked when the power will come back. If there is an evacuation, you will be asked when people can return to their homes. If the CEO has been accused of unethical behavior, you will be asked when they will step down. Sounds simple? Then tell me why so many officials look like a deer in headlights when asked about them. Do you know why? I can answer that one too. Because too many leaders and spokespersons like to focus on the key messages and avoid the challenging questions. Key messages are important, but that process is bass ackwards. Sometimes they do not want to address them because the questions and answers are embarrassing internally, let alone externally. Remind them what Oscar Wilde said, "Questions are never indiscreet ...." More importantly, remind them that the ramifications of not thinking about these and preparing responses to query is a far greater risk.

While I was a spokesperson in Puerto Rico, responding to Hurricane Maria, we learned that some of the food packages included more candy than nutrition. Skittles. We knew we would get questions. Before the first reporter called, we did our homework and prepared an answer that acknowledged there were, in fact, food packages with candy, but there was also an abundance of hot and cold nutritious food available at a multitude of locations and that the amount of food we were providing was historic in nature. We assured them that the candy had already been identified, removed, and replaced and that even more food was on its way to every single municipality. We vowed to workday and night to ensure everyone who needed help would have it and we backed that up. We published a statement. We publicized all the feeding locations. And we put videos on Facebook showing survivors receiving the hot meals. We still took some hits in the media, and we deserved them, but not as many as we would have endured if we did not anticipate the questions.

Predict the worst questions and develop the best answers.

That does not mean you have to answer every question. You may have heard of that classic question dilemma, "have you stopped beating your wife?" Whether you answer yes or no to that it is a losing situation. Some questions are wrong. Some are insulting. Some are inappropriate. Some have nothing to do with a more urgent life-saving discussion that should be happening. Some might be seeking classified information. Some may violate the Privacy Act.

You do not have to *answer* every question, but I do believe we should *address* every question. In the instances above, simply explain why their question is not appropriate and then tell them things you can tell them. Avoid the "no comment," response since historically that makes you look like you are hiding something.

I get asked about it all the time. What do I say when I cannot comment if I cannot say I cannot comment?

One word. **Segue.** Some people prefer the word bridge or bridging. The word is not as important as the concept. To segue or bridge is to move without interruption from one scene to another. I prefer "segue" because it is a cool sounding word and a homophone (spelled differently, pronounced the same, and have different meanings) to "segway," the transport device. Whenever I need to segue, I mentally picture the segway waiting to transport the conversation to a different place.

Segues take practice. The key to success is to make them seamless, without interruption or awkwardness. Here is an example of a poorly done segue:

Reporter: *"What do you say to people who will ask where FEMA is since you didn't show up for Katrina?"*

Response: *"We did too show up in Katrina. Anyway, in this case, we have not had any complaints from the state."*

Not good. Not good at all. In late summer 2008, I was the Acting and Deputy Director of Public Affairs at FEMA. I had only been in the position for about two months and our agency was responding to Hurricanes Ike and Gustav that struck the Gulf Coast. I could barely retain all the acronyms, let alone, have a solid foundation of intricate program deliverables. I was working at our HQs in Washington, DC one morning when a member of the staff told me there was some kind of problem outside the front doors of the building and that the Director wanted me to go out there and "handle" it. In hindsight, I should have asked more questions, but instead I made my way without delay. As I stepped outside, I was immediately confronted by several camera crews, reporters and microphones. On a national live feed someone pushed a microphone in front of my face and actually asked me that question. But I did not respond like the example above, because I know, value, and train on using segues. Instead, it went like this:

Reporter: *"What do you say to people who will ask where FEMA is since you didn't show up for Katrina?"*

Dan Stoneking: *"When people ask me where FEMA is, I invite them to look to their left and look to their right. FEMA was on the ground in Texas and Louisiana before, during, and since landfall, working side by side with state counterparts to save lives and sustain property. We have 840 people on the ground right now and more on the way. Let me highlight some of the things we have done to this point...."*

I use the examples above to also highlight another principle, ***avoid negatives.*** The obvious negatives are no, not, never, did not, could not, and so forth. If you are asked why you failed to put proper safety policies in place and you respond by saying you did not *fail*, you have just empowered the reporter to print X official claims not to have *failed* in safety policies." Most people cannot or do not actually hear the denial. All that registers is the repetition of the negative that they then associate with the speaker. It is always better to respond with a positive. In this case, explaining that you have a great safety record, solid safety policies, and that people and their safety are paramount in your organization. And then segue, of course.

Negatives are not always as obvious as those words that would be considered negative in any environment. When I was Deputy Director for Public Affairs at the National Guard Bureau, I instructed the team never to use the term "weekend warrior," even when refuting it. Those words are an insult to the people who fight for and protect their country. Likewise, in my FEMA role, I asked the staff not to use the word, "Katrina." Note that I did not use it in my reply above. Fair or not, that word will always be associated with a negative perception of FEMA. If I managed a restaurant that had a problem with rat infestation (see, just saying that is horribly negative), I could talk all day about our improved hygiene standards, the quality of training we are giving our staff, and our commitment to cleanliness. All without saying the "r" word.

One last principle that should not only be instilled in the entire organization, but also actually taught to everyone in the organization might sound simple but is a bit more complex than you might think. ***Do not lie.***

We all lie. That is nothing new. We lie so we do not hurt someone's feelings. To avoid embarrassment. To impress others. To avoid trouble. To protect a friend. Those are the lies we tell on *purpose*. Conscious choice. I cannot help you with that. But we also lie unintentionally.

Some will claim that these are not actually lies because no deceit was intended. Others have referred to them as "honest lies," which is both an oxymoron and a bit of an obfuscation. For our purposes here, let us consider a lie as saying something that is not true. Because in personal and professional environments, and especially with the media, nobody ever circles back to acknowledge, "Oh, all good, he didn't really intend to say that." The damage is done once it leaves our lips. We do not get forgiven for unintentionally not paying our mortgage. We are not forgiven when we unintentionally cause a car accident. With mortgages and cars, we learn in advance how to protect ourselves. We should do the same with what we say. Here are some examples of how we lie without intention.

By Confirmation. There was an old television show called "Columbo." It was about this detective who always seemed a bit hapless, but in reality, he was pretty shrewd. He had this habit in every episode of asking a witness several questions, claiming he was done, and then he started to walk away. Just before he departed, he would turn back and ask one last random question. Invariably the witness would be so desperate for that fleeting escape they would confirm anything. That is where he always got them. In media interviews this often manifests in an analogous way when an interview is going well and towards the end. the reporter seeks assurance with a phrase that begins like "Oh, by the way, it's true isn't it, that…?" I do not think they are being malicious. They just want to double-check a detail. Then the interviewee, who up to that point has done great, wants to please, and says something like, "Yes, I think that's right." That is the nail in the coffin. The solution here is simple - never confirm anything. If asked to confirm something, simply restate the issue from your perspective based on what you know personally. Or have the courage to say you do not know. I have done that hundreds of times and I am still standing.

By Assumption. Do you know what you do when you assume? You make an ass, um, well you know. I will be fair and humble here and use one of my mistakes as an example. I like visuals, so I asked our logisticians to send me pictures of trucks arriving at the field distribution center. In the course of the day, I was emailed the photos, added a caption to them, and posted them to social media. I thought I had done due diligence. An hour later, I heard in a briefing that the trucks would be arriving in three hours. I interrupted claiming that was not possible because I have photos that showed they arrived. That is when I learned that the photos were of the trucks departing from their original location, not arriving at the new one. Ugh. My co-workers teased me quite a bit about that one and I deserved it.

By Accident. We all make mistakes. But when it comes to our word, we should be twice as careful. There are reasons why Search and Rescue professionals may call off a search. But you do not hear them say that there are no living people still trapped or missing. Because they do not know. That topic is so sensitive and tragic that they are hyper alert about what they can say or not say. A common lie by accident in a crisis is when a spokesperson uses data from a dated operational report without including the date and time of the information. For example, one might brief the media that only 17% of the impacted area is without power. But if a reporter has seen a more current report that the number has increased to 31%, the speaker loses credibility.

By Statistic. "In 2007, toothpaste company Colgate ran an ad stating that 80% of dentists recommend their product. Based on the promotion, many shoppers assumed Colgate was the best toothpaste choice for their dental health."[36] That was clearly the implication. In reality, the survey asked respondents to list several brands of toothpaste they would recommend. We never learn the percentage of dentists who recommend other brands. A lie is a lie even if it is a lie of omission. Not cool. And Colgate's reputation suffered for a bit. Statistics are often used in a crisis. Hurricane Ida in 2021 was costlier than Hurricane Maria in 2016.[37] Sounds like Ida was worse, until you learn that varied reports estimate about one hundred deaths due to Ida, but more than 3,000 due to Maria. Which sounds worse now? No two crises are the same and to compare them or use statistics without context may create a whole new crisis, this time with trust.

By Quoting a Lie (Without Citation). The most common way I have seen this is when otherwise intelligent and seasoned communicators quote something that was reported in the media on air or print, without citing the source. That is a dangerous practice because the media makes mistakes, and you are risking your good word on their accuracy. If the Kansas City Star reports that three tornadoes touch down and you then use that as your own information, you are taking a

---

[36] *"Five Sources of Misleading Statistics,"* Geckoboard
[37] *"Facts and Statistics: Hurricanes,"* Insurance Information Institute

substantial risk and may be lying by quoting a source you have not cited. Then it becomes your words. Hard to explain later what you said when there were, in fact, only two tornadoes. I bet many of you are reading this and thinking nobody would make that mistake. Unfortunately, I have seen it and corrected it more times than I care to count. Cite the source.

By Speculation. I worked for a strong, bold, and intelligent boss several years ago, who was implementing a housing plan in a devastated community. He wanted me to tell the media that we would have forty temporary homes in place and occupied by the end of the month. I had not been at the organization long, but I knew enough to be aware that we did not always achieve our bold goals. I pushed back. He was not happy, but he relented. At the end of the month, we were able to tell the truth, and a good news story, about the thirty-four homes that had been completed. Had we stuck with the original idea, we would have lied by speculation and the success would have seemed like a failure.

Commit to speaking with intention and you will never make a mistake again. Okay, that was a lie. I am going to tell another lie today to get out of a social commitment. Us introverts do this often. At least I am telling a lie on purpose, and I am prepared for the consequences.

Anticipate. Segue. Avoid negatives. Do not lie. Be intentional. Become an expert on each of these and you can move on to the actual questions.

3 Feet

On the fourth day of a crisis, you are feeling good because you have answered the anticipated questions, and you have a rhythm going. You grant an interview to a national reporter, and they sit down with your boss and begin asking questions. You are comfortable because you put together a great prep package and established all the necessary ground rules. At that moment, can you say that you are even more secure because you are also an expert on the *eight types of questions*, and you have trained your boss on them as well? Uh oh. You should be an expert on these. The reporter is. They learned them in the first semester of journalism school. They have learned many more types, but these are the eight that I see asked frequently but are not always answered thoughtfully. Here is the good news. You are not on the fourth day. The crisis has not happened yet. You are sitting here reading this book. More good news - you cannot pick the questions, but you *can* pick the answers and you can shape the environment as you recognize and become an expert at responses to these types of questions. I will define each here and follow them individually with an example of how to effectively resolve.

Hypothetical: These are the "What if…' questions and they try to pull you into speculation, which we now know is a pitfall. The solution is to not take the bait. Restate the reality and segue (we always segue). Let us have some fun and not make these examples related to dark and sad events. The challenges and the resolutions are ubiquitous. These might be more fun and memorable.

Q: What would you do first if you were made king of the world?
A: Well, I am not the king of the world. I am the manager here at McDonald's and I love it. Let me tell you about our new menu item….

False Facts/Assumptions: These are questions that include false information, potentially false information, or assumptions. Call them out. Correct them. Protect your credibility.

Q: Nobody likes horror movies and the Director's Guild said you are wasting your career staying in this genre. Why don't you try to make a more meaningful type of movie?
A: On the contrary, I get fan mail all the time and the theaters are always packed. I am not personally aware of what the Director's Guild did or did not say, but each movie I direct has great

depth and meaning. For example, the movie I am directing now....

Leading: These are common with lawyers, but investigative journalists love them too. A leading question suggests a particular answer that the questioner desires. That answer is usually yes or no. Do not be led. Do not answer with just a yes or no. Try to avoid them and add context. You are in an interview, not a court of law, so no one is going to call an objection.

Q: You were the last one to leave the bar that night, weren't you?
A: I do not make a habit of tracking people in front of me or behind me. I left the bar at 11:30 pm. It is my understanding that the bar does not close until midnight, so I would have no information on who might have been there later. By that time, I was home with my wife watching Jimmy Fallon. He had the funniest guest....

Forced Question: These try to compel respondents to select an option that reflects their experience or opinion. Sometimes they are clear, reasonable, and you have a strong opinion to share. If so, go for it. But if they paint you into a corner that you do not want, you simply do not have to follow their rule and choose.

Q: Are you for or against the Oxford comma?
A: I am in favor of using punctuation to convey

meaning. If they accomplish that, then they have done their job well. In fact, I authored a paper on this I can share….

Factual: These are typically direct and clear, without hidden agenda. The mistake respondents tend to make here is that they are so relieved, they only give the short, clear and direct answer without context. Add context that is helpful to your efforts and perspective.

Q: What percentage of donations go to overhead and administrative costs as opposed to the actual medical research?
A: In order to maintain the staff and resources to be effective, we are obligated to apportion 6% of donations to the administrative costs that support people who are working hard every day to find a cure. We have an independent auditing firm that ensures that we are fiscally responsible, and we are completely transparent on our budget. This enables us to accomplish amazing breakthroughs like….

Cannot Answer: There are many questions that you will not be able to answer for a wide array of reasons. Classified. Under Investigation. Simply do not know. The important thing to remember is to not say "no comment" or "I can't answer that." Aside from being negative, they are just not helpful.

Q: Is it true that Frank Abagnale committed fraud as he posed as a pilot of a major airline, and later as a surgical doctor?

A: The case is still under investigation, but I can tell you that we are pursuing this with vigor and if Mr. Abagnale is found guilty, we will pursue this to the fullest extent of the law. Anyone impersonating a pilot or doctor puts people at significant risk....

Opinion: These questions want to know what you think, or how you feel. The problem is that any opinion you give will reflect on the entire organization. That can be dangerous since an individual's opinions do not align 100% with their employers. It is always best to avoid opinions. But similar to the "no comment" rule, avoid saying that you are not going to give your opinion. It comes off as defensive.

Q: How do you feel about your company developing these new lines of widgets in assorted sizes and colors? Are you worried that this would burden the manufacturing team with the sudden shift in supply and demand?

A: Wally's Widgets has been in business long before I was born, and I am sure they will still be thriving long after I am gone. As long as I am here, I am just excited to be making high-quality widgets. Would you like to see our latest line...?

Softball: These are the ones that are supposed to be extremely easy to answer. They are tossing you a softball. Easy to catch. They often come as the last question. They are common in job interviews as well as media interviews. Give me a second to vent here. I feel like I should not even have to explain how to answer an easy question, but I do because I have been so frustrated by how often I see this one screwed up. Ugh. Sorry. Since people mess it up so much, I will give two examples. In each, I will give the common Wrong Answer (WA) and the Right Answer (RA).

Q: Well, thanks for coming in to interview for the job. Do you have anything else to add?
WA: No. Thank you.
RA: Yes! First, I want to thank all of you for taking the time to speak with me today. Having heard your feedback, this job is a perfect and mutually beneficial fit. I am not applying for *any* job; I want *this* job. And I hope I have convinced you of my passion and what I bring to the table. If you want any more information at any time, please do not hesitate to reach out. I look forward to hearing from you soon so we can do remarkable things together!

Q: We understand that you are dealing with a crisis, so we will not waste any more of your time, unless you have anything else to share.

WA: Thanks. I will get back to work now.

RA: This interview is important. The community needs to know what is going on. So, I want to share and stress: Key Message. Key Message. Key Message.

You do not have to answer every question; but you must address them. By understanding the types of questions, you and your principals are more empowered to provide honest, intentional, and effective responses that shape the environment.

These first eight chapters are the seeds. Water them. Nurture them.

###

Branches

In time, branches will spread out near and far from the trunk. They will be different in size and shape. They are secondary to the main axis, but just as essential for life and growth. They are part of something bigger than themselves. Sometimes they need to be pruned, other times they need to extend in different directions. In this part, we will examine the internal tools and external relationships that expand your programs from simply functioning organisms into thriving canopies with a compelling impact.

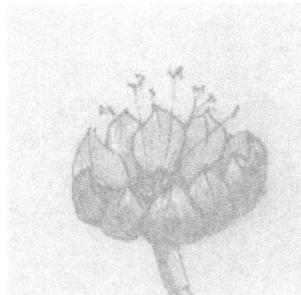

Chapter 9   Social Media

"There are positive things that come of social media as well as negative."
-   Millie Bobby Brown

"We become what we behold. We shape our tools and then our tools shape us."
-   Marshall McLuhan

"One of my mottos is 'the right tool for the right job."
-   Martha Stewart

Chapter 9   Social Media by Rebecca
Kuperberg

Introduction

I am a millennial. One of the defining
characteristics of my generation is that I "came of
age during the internet explosion."[38] The iPhone
launched when I was nine years old, though it
would be many more years before I had my first
smartphone. I remember the sound of the dial-up
connection and opening my first Facebook
account when I started college, back when you
needed a .edu email address to register for the
platform.

I remember enough of the world before
smartphones and 5G internet to remain in awe of
the internet. We walk around all day with access
to more knowledge in our back pockets than
exists in libraries and museums. As a kid, I had
international pen pals. I wrote letters and waited
weeks and months for a response. Now, I text
with friends in Hong Kong and England with the
press of a button, our messages sending and
receiving instantly. I even live streamed my

---

[38] Where Millennials end and Generation Z begins |
Pew Research Center

wedding to friends and family around the world who could not be there in person.

But, like everyone on the internet, I am also deeply aware of the downsides of this hyperconnectivity. As a graduate student, I researched online violence against women politicians. The majority of abuse and harassment of public officials online takes place on commonly used social media platforms like X (formerly Twitter), Facebook, Instagram, and WhatsApp. I have seen family members fall victim to online frauds and read stories of everyday people, especially children and young adults, subjected to online bullying with few resources to protect themselves.

Is social media good or bad? This question is beyond the scope of this book, and I am not the best person to answer it. Is social media good or bad for emergency management? Both. Social media is a tool to get a message out. That tool can be used well and poorly. It can be received well or poorly. And it can be taken advantage of. But importantly, there are actions we can all take, personally and professionally, to shift the scale. When done well, social media can help us communicate with the public quickly, reliably, and safely.

30,000 Feet: The ugly, the bad, and the good

The ugly

Moments after the horrific elementary school shooting in Uvalde, Texas, in May 2022, social media users posted their theories. Some claimed it was a government conspiracy to push for gun control while others claimed that the shooter was an undocumented immigrant.[39] After violent events, online posts do not just stay online. In the aftermath of a 2023 knife attack outside an elementary school in Dublin, Ireland, hundreds started to riot, driven by false claims on social media that the attacker was an immigrant.[40] This first emergency, a school stabbing, prompted another emergency. Police vehicles and shops were damaged; police officers were injured. Social media can be ugly. And it can contribute to, even create, emergencies offline.

---

[39] The Texas school shooting conspiracies show far-right misinformation is evolving : NPR
[40] Dublin riot saw most riot police deployed in Irish state history (bbc.com)

Before we continue, there are a couple of words it is useful to define: disinformation and misinformation. Misinformation is false or misleading information. Disinformation is the *intentional* creation and spreading of false information.

Disinformation is part of *the ugly* side of social media. Bad actors sow confusion, chaos, and even violence by deliberately creating and sharing false information. Disinformation was seen at a large scale in the emergency management world in response to COVID-19. Individuals seeking to profit from fear and anxiety shared dangerous remedies and encouraged the public not to trust doctors and other official sources. We are still feeling the effects of this disinformation with other vaccine rates, like the flu vaccine, lower than pre-pandemic levels. And though the pandemic offers a clear illustration of disinformation's downsides, disinformation can impact other types of emergencies as seen in the example from Ireland above.

Violence and threats are another aspect of social media's *ugly side.* Nobody is immune from harassment and violence online, including local government officials, public health workers, and emergency managers. In times of stress, such as emergencies, violence and threats online tend to get worse.

None of these issues—disinformation, violence, and threats—are unique to the internet or social media. But, on social media, individuals from anywhere in the world can share information online and posts can go viral, spreading rapidly across the internet, whether they are truthful or false. Platforms like X (formerly Twitter) can also, intentionally and unintentionally, promote violent and inflammatory posts so that they reach more people.

The bad

If disinformation is the ugly, misinformation is the bad. Even though internet users are not sharing false information with the intention to cause harm, misinformation still creates confusion, sows mistrust, and helps the rapid spread of falsehoods. It may be one person who writes a post intending to cause harm, but it can be hundreds or thousands who spread it.

Misinformation can cause members of the public to lose trust in facts and official sources. In turn, officials can lose control of the narrative. Regaining trust is often challenging and can take time, time that might not exist in the context of an evolving emergency. It might seem logical to ignore these false stories. Responding to false information seems like giving it a platform or some type of legitimacy. But more false information will fester and grow to fill a vacuum of silence online.

FEMA has had success with webpages and social media posts devoted to debunking rumors online. Rather than let rumors and falsehoods grow, the agency tracks rumors and responds to them, regaining control of the message.

The good
With all that can go wrong online, what is the point? Might it be better just to avoid social media altogether?

Social media has downsides, but it also has advantages. And these advantages are specific to social media. We cannot just take the same messages we would share on Facebook or Instagram and put them on a website or give them to the media. Sharing information on social media is quick, requires little cost, requires little effort, and meets people where they are. The public is on social media. Communities are looking for answers online and in the absence of trustworthy information, will turn to untrustworthy information because it is there.

Social media allows for messages to be shared instantaneously. Gone are the days when members of the public had to wait for the morning paper or rush to get home to turn on a tv or radio for information they need. And information can be updated quickly. Growing up in southern California, we would turn into the local news to keep an eye on wildfire boundaries and evacuations. I remember watching the same information over and over again until the newscasters were given new and updated data. Now, living across the country, I can go to the California Department of Forestry and Fire Protection (CAL FIRE)'s Facebook page and see changes to the fire boundaries as soon as the information is published.

Emergency managers can record videos, share maps, release messages, and share images quickly and cheaply and can reach community members where they are. Eighty-one percent of U.S. adults have a Facebook account. Less than one-third of American households have an operational landline phone. To share messages effectively, they must be clear and timely. But they also have to be transmitted effectively. And almost nothing is more effective at reaching the general public than social media.

Finally, social media also allows for exchange. Emergency managers can put out messages and updates and respond, in real time, to questions and clarifications. Users can go on social media to share reports of damage, point to blocked roads, downed power lines, or other hazards, and alert authorities to people in need. Social media is not only important because it allows messages to go out quickly and cheaply; it also brings messages in.

Three Feet

There are things we can all do, professionally as emergency managers and personally as internet users, to make social media platforms work better for us. Here are some of those things:

Make good choices
Social media platforms are not all created equal. Each has a different audience and format. You

may be familiar with these platforms from your personal, or other professional, life. But familiarity is not necessarily a reason to choose one platform over another.

Platforms are not a one-size-fits-all. In some areas of the U.S., X or LinkedIn may have a wide reach. In others, residents might use Facebook for staying connected. For some communities, an email chain or text chain could be a better option.

Though this will list will change soon, here is some information about the most common platforms now:

X (formerly Twitter):
- Pros: Historically, used to share breaking news and emergency alerts. Used by political professionals and public figures.
- Cons: Most posts can now only be viewed with an account. Limited moderation following new ownership.

Facebook:
- Pros: Wide user base though tends to skew older. Part of a suite of platforms including Instagram and Threads. Information on public Facebook pages is

usually viewable by users who do not have an account making it easier to share information widely. Videos and livestreams can be hosted on Facebook, so they do not need to be imported from other platforms.
- Cons: Young people are less likely to use Facebook though more likely to use Instagram.

NextDoor:
- Pros: Neighborhood-based platform that allows for targeted messaging to a particular area. Users turn to this platform for emergency management-related information such as road closures and emergency alerts.
- Cons: A limited demographic that may not reach vulnerable populations or individuals outside of a specified neighborhood. Information can be hard to access without an account.

Train

There are many great resources, many of them free or low-cost, to gain social media skills. While having personal experience using an app or platform is broad knowledge to bring to a professional setting, it is not usually enough. Seek out training and encourage training for colleagues and staff to make the most out of social media.

Make a plan

Rather than wait for bad actors to spam accounts, try to hack into accounts, or abuse staff, make a plan for how to deal with incidents before they take place. Plans should consider the safety of staff, how to regain trust with the audience, and account security.

Protect

While it is great to have multiple staff running an account, the more people who have a username and password, the greater the chance an account will be hacked. Options like multi-factor authentication offer added protection. Other best practices include using a secure internet connection, keeping applications and systems updated, and being familiar with common frauds.

Be genuine

Over the summer, there was a flash flood that impacted my township and neighboring townships. Unfortunately, this resulted in loss of life including, devastatingly, the loss of two children. The township Fire Chief posted updates on Facebook, including video updates. He shared the facts but was also open about the emotional toll of this incident on the community and on the fire department. He became *the* trusted community messenger for information. And it was not just because he shared updates. He showed that he cared.

There is no turning back. We live in a world with social media. The platforms may change, the filters may become more realistic. But we turn to social media platforms to get information and stay connected. This is one of our most valuable tools, so long as we harness it correctly.

###

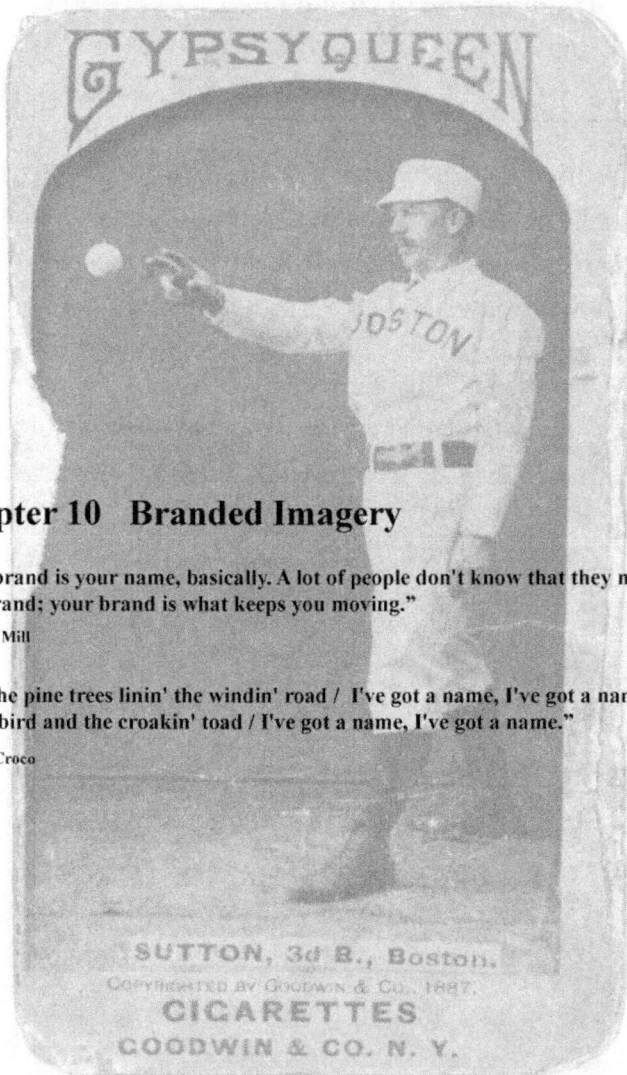

Chapter 10   Branded Imagery

"Your brand is your name, basically. A lot of people don't know that they need to build their brand; your brand is what keeps you moving."

- Meek Mill

"Like the pine trees linin' the windin' road / I've got a name, I've got a name / Like the singin' bird and the croakin' toad / I've got a name, I've got a name."

- Jim Croco

Chapter 10   Branded Imagery by Dan Stoneking

"In January 1996, I was watching the Superbowl between the Dallas Cowboys and the Pittsburgh Steelers. As a life-long Minnesota Viking fan, I was not that invested in the outcome. Like many Americans, I was in it for the commercials. When one of the breaks occurred, I found myself watching a baby in her swing. She is happy, and then sad. Happy, and then sad. At the end of the commercial it is revealed that on the upswings, she sees the McDonald's Golden Arches sign outside the window she is facing. And on the downswings, it is gone. No word was ever spoken.[41] I thought to myself, wow, powerful on so many levels.

It showed me that great imagery does not always need words. The intent was eminently clear. It also showed that branding can be so visual, so powerful, that even an infant can associate it with something greater. I began my career in communications a few years later, but that has always stayed with me. It is also the reason behind the title of this chapter and my philosophy. There are books and articles written about branding and separately there are even more written about imagery, photography, and

---

[41] *"McDonald's Baby Swing Ad, 1996,"* YouTube

videography. I think separating the two minimizes their combined power and leads people to forget that they are inextricably intertwined. Branding should always consider imagery and imagery should always consider branding. Hence, the branded imagery approach.

30,000 Feet

In 2023, a pseudo-political discord occurred in our society over country singer Jason Aldean's song, *Try That in a Small Town.* Let us skip past the pedantic issue of liberal versus conservative narrative for a moment and focus on two interesting and unrelated lessons of crisis communications that this song highlights: communities and imagery and how they coalesce.

Whether he realized it, or not, Aldean was loosely applying a sociological construct that a German author, Ferdinand Tönnies coined, called Gemeinschaft and Gesellschaft.[42] Tönnies makes a distinction between the Gemeinschaft (communal society) and the Gesellschaft (associational society). Gemeinschafts, or small towns, are regulated by traditional social roles, natural emotions, and expressions of sentiment. The Gesellschaft, or cosmopolitan societies, in contrast, are governed by bureaucracies and

---

[42] *"Who was Ferdinand Tonnies?"* Study.com

industrial societies that are less personal and –
one could certainly argue – weaken the
traditional bonds of family and kinship.

Aldean would not get any complaints from either
liberals or conservatives that there is much to be
said about the differences in culture between
small towns and mass society. Tönnies beat him
to the punch on that point, but Aldean's
comparison in that regard is not what contributed
to a crisis here. And let me interrupt myself to
point out that this meets a criterion or two for a
crisis since it has resulted in some negative
impact to his reputation, his ability to air his
music on some country platforms, and the
growing divide in society. The first contribution
to the crisis is Aldean's misperception that all
small towns are the same. They clearly are not.
The values and emotions of towns like Hereford,
Texas and Sumiton, Alabama are vastly different
than those of Williston, VT and El Cerrito,
California, as a few examples. What goes over
well in one of those former towns will not be
acceptable in the latter ones and vice versa.
Imagery can provoke different emotions from
different audiences, different communities.

Maybe what Aldean meant to say was [don't] try
that in *my* small town. If that is the case, he is
already alienating other small towns, not just big
cities and society. For that matter, what does he

even mean by "that?" Certainly, he lists a few examples, the sucker punch on a sidewalk, the carjacking of an old lady, pulling a gun in a liquor store, cussing out a police officer, and stomping on and lighting up a flag. Is that the list? Does he mean to say that a) those five things collectively define "that?" and b) those are the five things you cannot do in a/his small town? Or does he mean that = violence? No. Rodeos can be violent. Playing chicken with two pick-up trucks on a country road can be violent. Does he mean that = illegal? Bootlegging is illegal. Lynching is illegal. He could have used hundreds of examples in his song. His choices must mean something. And here is where they say, let us go to the video.

Aldean's song and lyrics came out in May 2023,[43] while the video did not come out until July,[44] and it was only then that the debate began. I would suggest an exercise. In either order, read the lyrics and watch the video with the sound turned off. There is a pretty clear disconnect. It would be a great experiment to have a hundred people watch the video first without sound and be asked to say what the song is about. And a separate hundred people listen to the song first without video. I read the text first. Still, I was

[43] "'Try That in a Small Town' Lyrics," Genius
[44] "'Try That in a Small Town' Video," YouTube

confused when I saw the video. I felt the country boy bravado in the lyrics. But I felt sick when I watched the video. It was dark. But it was also confusing. There was a split-second image of a woman being hijacked. Way too fast and blurred to determine if she was old and whether she was at a red light. There were two quick images in a liquor store. And one swift image of a flag burning.

The song is about three minutes long. The vast majority of the video is showing protests, both violent and peaceful. Is that what *that* is? Is Aldean trying to tell us - to not try to protest in his town? The word protest never appears in his lyrics. So why does it consume so much of the video? I do not know Aldean's intent, but it does demonstrate the power of imagery. It also shows that platitudes and pictures can tell a different story. When the song was first playing on the radio, we heard little discontent. But as the music video made the rounds, the complaints grew. That alone is evidence enough that they elicited different emotions.

I am neither outraged nor interested in this music video. The conservative versus liberal tug of war here is blatantly self-evident, indulgent, and blasé. I do not know Jason Aldean's intent here and it really does not matter to me. But the juxtaposition of communities and the juxtaposition of imagery and words are powerful examples of factors that every crisis communicator should consider. *His* imagery contradicted *his* words, and negatively impacted *his* brand. Another solid argument for a branded imagery approach.

Since both of those stories are video examples of imagery, let us assess a few photographs as well. They may lack the motion but are still full of emotion.

In 1972, Nick Ut, a young and new journalist, took a photo, "Napalm Girl," of children running down the street, one of them naked, suffering from napalm burns and running for their lives after bombing during the Vietnam War. Nick earned a Pulitzer Prize for the photo because the imagery was so painful, many credit the image as a turning point to end the war.[45]

A year later, another iconic photo, "Burst of Joy," earned photographer Slav Veder a Pulitzer prize as well, as it came to symbolize the end of the same Vietnam War. That photo shows Lt. Col. Robert L. Stirm, after spending more than five years in a North Vietnamese camp, reunited with his family at Travis Air Force Base.[46]

---

[45] *"Story of 'Napalm Girl,'"* About Photography Blog
[46] *"Burst of Joy,"* Rare Historical Photos

I share these two photos, related to similar content for a few reasons. First, I think many of you will recall them, even if you were not alive then. If you do not from my description, you will once you look at them. Feel free to pause here and search them on the internet.   I am sure they will evoke emotions. These photos impacted a generation. Yet, the truth behind each may surprise you. The horrific image of the young girl might lead you to believe that she perished soon after. In fact, she went on to lead a full and happy life. The image of the officer and his family will fill you with joy and yet, the image caused the officer pain for many years afterwards because he received a letter from his wife just a few days before requesting a divorce, and their family broke up soon after.

These examples remind us that images are a *snapshot in time*. The stories, the people, and the meanings can change. The Subway fast-food chain published countless photos and videos of Jared Fogle as a spokesperson for their product. In 2015, Fogle was sentenced to federal prison for child sex crimes. Subway suffered from their choices in branded imagery.

You might ask why I used photos from the 1970's. They may seem dated. I wanted to show how enduring imagery can be. But, in addition to that, it was difficult to find anything iconic from the last twenty years. Okay, there is that one *selfie*-photo that Ellen Degeneres took during the March 2014 Oscar ceremony in Los Angeles.[47]

> *(Allow me this parenthetical. I made up a word that is now used frequently. You may have used it yourself. "Ussie." I am a literal person and always found it annoying when two or more people took a photo together and defined it singularly as a "selfie." So, I fixed it. If you do an internet search you will likely find that the word has been around "at least since April 2013, according to Ben Zimmer, executive producer of Vocabulary.com and language columnist for The Wall Street Journal." I do not know Ben. More importantly, Ben does not know me. But I was smart enough to start posting and labeling my self-described ussies on Facebook as early as 2011. I have a bunch of Facebook friends who can verify. They are all the evidence I need. And the ussies, of course, with my daughters, Ivy Grace and Chloe Lane. They are so cute.)*

---

[47] *"The Most Famous Selfies of All Time,"* Hackernhttps://hackernoon.com/the-most-famous-selfies-of-all-time-2480023beb5coon

But Ellen's *selfie* lacked any real storytelling. It lacked emotion aside from a quick grin. If I referred to the napalm girl, everyone in my generation would know the reference. Everyone felt the same angst. Can you name one photograph taken in the last twenty years, apart from Ellen's, that you could mention to anyone, and they would recognize? Can you name the last Pulitzer Prize winning photograph? Me either.

Photography has evolved. Everyone who has a smartphone is a photographer. We are gaining more access to more images drawn from more places and times in the world than ever before. Photographic technology has enabled images to be copied and mass-distributed at unparalleled rates. That may weaken them in a historical context, but it does not weaken them at the moment. Just ask the last "Karen" that got fired from her job.

Your brand is your image; your image is your brand.

Three Feet

I have no interest, inclination, nor education to teach anyone how to manually set the white balance, adjust the shutter speed, or set the aperture. The photographers and videographers who collaborate with you are experts on their equipment. They do, however, need to be pulled into the strategic and tactical purposes for the imagery. Too often in a crisis I see photographers let out into the field, sans guidance, to take images they see fit, without the context of the rest of the mission and the desired outcomes. A few stories can bring this point to life.

The National Guard.

In 2007, as the Deputy Director of Public Affairs for the National Guard Bureau (NGB). The three-star general, Chief of NGB, put me to a challenge on an upcoming national exercise in Camp Atterbury, IN, where we would be collaborating with active duty Army units in a crisis response scenario. The Chief told me that he wanted the media and the world to know our motto, "Always Ready, Always There" and that he also wanted them to know our key message that the National Guard is the first *military* responder in any crisis, not the Army, Air Force, Navy, or Marines.

I took the challenge. First, we made hundreds of magnets and decals in assorted sizes that included our minuteman image and our motto. We put them on every vehicle, tent, and piece of equipment we deployed there. We made a pop-up backdrop for media availability with the same. When the time came for the exercise, I embedded national media on a flight with us from Washington, DC to Indiana, where we would then join with our active Army counterparts. I provided every member of the media with a press packet that included several pages of fact sheets and exercise information. On each page on the bottom and in bold italics were the words *"The National Guard is the First Military Responder."* I had the Chief brief them during the flight and I asked him to deftly repeat that phrase at least five times during the two-hours en route. Upon arrival, we coordinated to do a joint press brief with the Army General, where our Chief spoke first, repeated the mantra again, and then turned to his counterpart and said, "Isn't that right?" He agreed. We captured it all in countless photographs and videos. On the flight home, I provided the media with b-roll and asked them directly to reinforce our latest mantra.

That night, when I heard the CNN correspondent actually open his segment with those very words, while our video showed several examples of our magnets and stickers, I knew I had passed the test.

FEMA.

A few years later, as the Deputy Director of Public Affairs for FEMA, I was deployed to American Samoa responding to a tsunami and earthquake. Response and recovery were going well, but a few days into our efforts,

Congressional Members in California were making claims that the citizens were without food and groceries, which simply was not true. Instead of debating in words, I grabbed one of our senior officials and a videographer and we went to one of the large stores where all of the shelves were fully stocked. We added b-roll that showed feeding sites, and other commodities as part of a multi-pronged approach. The video proved that food and groceries were plentiful. We instantly sent it to our HQs in Washington, DC, who then posted it and shared it with Members of Congress.[48] We never heard from the California delegation again. Solved. Done. And by the way, I had the senior official wear his FEMA shirt. Branded Imagery.

In neither of these examples, or any time in my career, did I touch a camera, still or video. I never advised anyone how to work the lighting. I did, however, in every crisis, give strategic guidance on what we needed to capture as well as feedback on products submitted. A few key elements stand out to me as areas most crisis communicators can improve with imagery

Strategic. Crisis communicators have a right and responsibility to tell the photographers and

---

[48] *"Disaster Supplies Are Meeting the Need in American Samoa,"* You Tube

videographers who, what, where, when, and why to capture. Often, in a crisis, this works best with a quick morning huddle and a mission assignment. Their tasks need to align with the story of the day. They must shoot, edit, and publish in a time limit that aligns with other products and messages. Where possible, assign multiple days.

Content. Tell the story. The story is not the crisis; it is the response to the crisis. I have seen far too many photographers come back with photos of flooding. The media is covering the flooding. Our job is to say and show how we are responding to the flooding. We do not want an image of the survivor standing in line. We want a picture of a Red Cross shirt and a FEMA shirt providing food or shelter. We do not want a picture of the CEO being led out in handcuffs. We want a picture of the Deputy CEO taking care of business in a conference room meeting. The lead communicator decides the content, not the photographer. The story is not the crisis; it is the response to the crisis.

Format. Most of your photographers will default to always coming to you with a batch of color photos. Next time, partly to see the look on their face, ask them what their strategic reasoning was for using color and not black and white. If they say anything like, well, that is the way we always do it, then you have a red flag. There are times when a black and white photograph can be powerful. The choice between the two should be strategic, not happenstance. Of course, the emerging option is Artificial Intelligence (AI) imager. There is another chapter coming up on AI in greater detail. Be thoughtful and deliberate on your decisions here. There are times and places where this avenue can provide you an image otherwise not available but be careful not to lose humanity. In addition, to ensure there are no ethical issues, credit every AI photo just as you would for a person, to avoid accusations of deception.

Captions. I like to say that great photos do not need a caption but include them anyway. But do not insult the audience by telling them what they are looking at, but rather explain what they do not see. For example, I have seen some amazing photographs of firefighters dealing with wildfires for several long days.

Bad example: *Unnamed firefighters taking a break during Mendocino Fire, July 2018*

Good example: *More than three hundred firefighters have been battling the Mendocino Fire without a day off for three weeks. Yet, none of them are complaining, July 2018*

In this book, I have included an original photograph with every chapter. I purposely did not caption any of them. After reading any or all of the chapters, go back and write that caption in a way that does not simply describe the image, but how it conveys, in some way, the content of the chapter it supports. It is a fun drill either individually, or for you to use with others. Again, these are original photographs. No one in the world has captioned them before. They are your tabula rasa.

Quantity. In the age of digital imagery, photographers and videographers should never return with three photos or three minutes of video. There should be fifty photos and thirty minutes of video. The cost is the same. Quantity gives them and the decision-makers more options.

Use it. I have seen whole days go by in a crisis without a photo or video being published. That is a wasted opportunity. Every useful imagery should be posted and pushed. Releases should include imagery. So should fact sheets. Social media should use them. Stakeholders should receive them.

Use it again. Both images and branding can be reused. Branding can be put on clothing, equipment, products, and email signature blocks.

Images can be linked to repeatedly. Images can be included in reports, meetings, presentations, and more. Think about where your branded imagery is seen as well as those gaps where they are not.

Storage. This may not be a fun part of the art of our business, but it is equally essential. In most organizations the storage capacity can be a limiting factor and yet the photographer has little to know power to resolve. Senior communicators must invest in solutions.

Transmission. Similarly, this is a technical issue, but needs to be addressed. Do not allow yourself to be in a position where you have an informative video to share, but the size of the file is preventing you. Whether it is the cloud, file-transfer-protocol, or some other solution, make sure **a)** you can transmit everything you need, **b)** everyone on your team knows how to do it, and **c)** the download for the recipient is clear and simple.

And always remember, the story is not the crisis; it is the response to the crisis.

One of the quotes that introduced this chapter was Quentin Tarantino saying, "When people ask me if I went to film school I tell them, 'no, I went to films.'" If you are not a photographer, you do not need to go to photography school. Go to photographs. Tell your story through branded imagery.

Your brand is your image; your image is your brand.

###

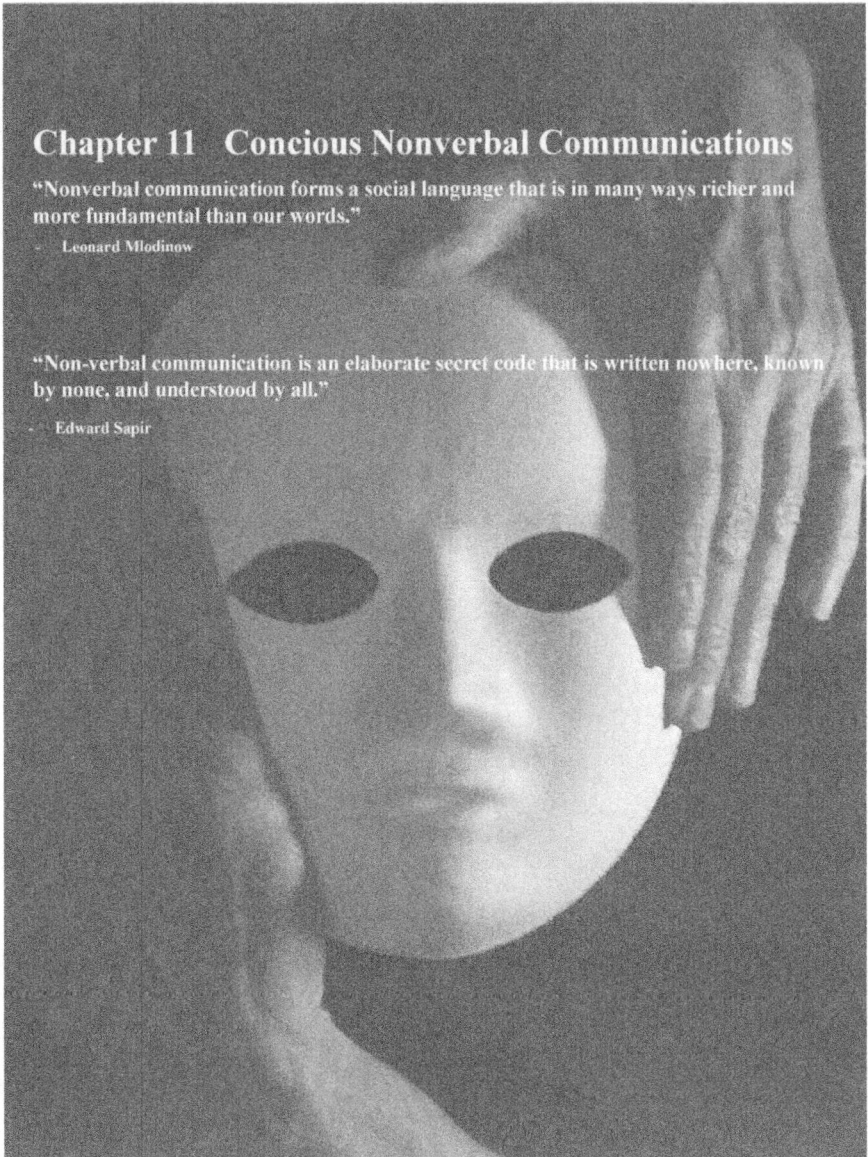

Chapter 11   Concious Nonverbal Communications

"Nonverbal communication forms a social language that is in many ways richer and more fundamental than our words."

- Leonard Mlodinow

"Non-verbal communication is an elaborate secret code that is written nowhere, known by none, and understood by all."

- Edward Sapir

Chapter 11   Conscious Nonverbal
Communications by Dan Stoneking

I told my daughter the other day, "It's not what you say, but how you say it." She tried to tell me that she could not help the way she sounded. I did not let her off the hook. Nonverbal communication is both conscious and unconscious, we express ourselves both intentionally and unintentionally. Conscious communication means that we think about our communication before we communicate. Unconscious communication means that we do not think about every message we communicate. I told my daughter to start thinking about it more. It is not always easy.

30,000 Feet

Brace yourself; it is always less about what we say than how we say it.

Have you ever had one of your kids in braces? It puts a bit of a dent in the piggy bank. I have had the older one in braces for three years, while the younger one has been wearing some kind of face guard that I do not fully understand. Now the older one is about to come out of braces just as the younger one goes into them. So, that expense will entertain me for about six long years. And there really is some entertainment. Their orthodontist sends regular emails to all us clients with nice pictures and often interesting factoids. Today's email shared the following:

What people most notice when meeting other people:

Smile	47%
Eyes	31%
Smell	11%
Clothes	7%
Hair	4%

With the smile coming in at a resounding first place, it is clear why the orthodontist shared this email. As someone who got braces as an adult, I can personally testify to the immense and obvious ways I have been treated differently before and after. All of the components above contribute to our physiology. Physiology combined with tone accounts for our Nonverbal Communications. According to the 7-38-55 rule, 93 percent of meaning is communicated nonverbally.[49]

Spoken Word	7%
Tone	38%
Physiology	55%

Think about how little even us professionals address nonverbals. For the spoken word, we

---

[49] *"How to Master the 7-38-55 Rule,"* Master Class Articles

have Talking Points. We do not have Tone Points. Or Physiology Points. We should. Think about your personal life. You can tell if your significant other is in a bad mood without either one of you uttering a word. And then you make a conscious choice to either try to help improve it, or quietly leave the room for a while. Conscious choice. We have all been around pets. We get signals to feed them, pet them, and walk them. And we choose to abide. Nonverbals are so powerful that they transcend species. But at work, even among us communication professionals, we seldom take the time to address nonverbals consciously and strategically for ourselves or others. We may not be able to invest 93% of our time addressing 93% of communications, but, with a little effort, we can become (and teach) conscious nonverbal communications by raising the bar from 0% to 5%.

Three Feet

As you read the following factors, try to pause after each one and think of yourself and another person. Identify a positive or negative example for each of you. If you are really motivated, even write them down so you can actually address them later.

Body Movement. Body movements are frequently indicators of self-confidence, energy, fatigue, or status. You have seen the speaker behind a lectern who scarcely moves at all. Yawn. Or the hyperactive one who may be entertaining, but so distracting that you miss the message. The key, like most of these, is to achieve balance and consciously ensure your movement is elevating your words. I have heard people advise others never to put their hands on a lectern. That is simply not true. Yes, gripping the lectern like a crutch and exposing your fear is too much. But there is little that you cannot do as long as you are being strategic and achieving the outcome you seek.

Gestures. Our gestures operate to clarify, contradict, or replace verbal messages. This is why people will use pointers during a visual presentation. Or hold up three fingers when you are emphasizing three main ideas. Clarification is good. Contradicting is bad. People will notice if you point to the wrong place on the map or address five points instead of the three you indicated.

Posture. Posture can indicate attitudes, moods, approval, deception, and warmth. You can lead forward in a chair and actively participate nonverbally, or slouch back and disengage. A simple short nod can let your partner know that you are following and good with what they are saying. A grimace will reveal the opposite. Be careful not to assume too much in what you see in others. They are called nonverbal clues, not nonverbal verifications. I have been told a thousand times that crossing your arms nonverbally suggests you are defensive. True. Sometimes. Sometimes not. Because I am aware of the possible interpretation, I try to avoid this habit. But I like crossing my arms. I got it from my Dad. I asked him why he did it, especially at times when I could see that he was happy and involved. "It's just comfortable," he said.

Face. Facial expressions can positively or negatively reinforce the spoken word too as they convey cues concerning emotions and attitude. Facial appearance also offers cues that reveal information like, age, sex, race, ethnic origin, and status. Some of those we cannot change, nor should we want to, but others we can. I used to prepare this one person for speaking engagements and I had to tell him that he always looked confused when people asked him questions. He explained to me that he was just thinking and processing. I told him that he was losing credibility and to stop it. He did. See, we can be conscious about this stuff.

Eyes. Our eyes provide a constant channel of communication. Poems have been written about them. They can be evasive; convey hate, fear, guilt; express confidence, love, support; can accurately indicate a positive or a negative relationship; and can indicate whether one is open to communication. Since I have stubbornly refused to accept my teenage daughters speaking to me in a rude tone, they have simply transitioned expressing their emotions to "the look." Ugh. Sometimes at work, I will play a power game with a colleague just for my own amusement. I will steadfastly keep looking right into their eyes until they flinch and look away. Try it.

Hands. I remember when COVID first started, I watched this doctor on television giving us all kinds of guidance. One of them was to refrain from touching our face, as we would spread germs. Before she completed her briefing, she had touched her face three times. I recently finished watching a television series called *"New Amsterdam."* In the last few episodes one of the prominent characters was deaf. Unlike other shows, she had several conversations that were not translated for us viewers. I could have put the caption on, but I marveled at their bold choice, and it made me pay greater attention. I was amazed at how much I could pick up. More importantly, it was a daring and conscious decision by the show's director that made those scenes much more compelling. Stop. Come. Enough. Question. Each of these can be prompted by our hands. Here is one you already use consciously if you are a communicator staffing a principal at a speaking engagement as time is running out - moving your hand, palm down, rapidly across your throat. Time to go boss. Like a catcher and pitcher in baseball, you can develop more of your own signals.

Appearance. If in that split second you saw the word "appearance" and thought that you always dress well, you missed the mark. Dressing well is not the goal. Dressing to achieve your desired outcome is the goal. Sometimes that means dressing more tactically in an austere environment. It is also why Presidents used to have fireside chats with the American public, so they would not come off overly officious. I had a friend who always wore a bow tie at work. I thought he had a cool, personal vibe. But, over time, he became known as the "bow tie guy,' and lost his audience focus.

Tone. Tone includes several individual traits like pace, inflection, pauses, repetition, energy, cadence, and articulation. To get in the habit of thinking about each of these more consciously, take a paragraph out of any novel. Read it the first time aloud however you would normally read it, your natural voice. The second time, keep changing up the pace. The third time, the inflection, etc. At the end, you will have spoken that paragraph eight separate ways. Now speak it one last time in the most effective, impactful way possible. The difference from your first to your last will be remarkable, especially if you can tape them and go back to compare. If you are training others, tone is very individualized. The slow talker needs to fix their pace. The one who mumbles needs to improve their articulation. Find each person's opportunity for improvement.

Here is another fun exercise for training – fill one box with dozens of examples of nonverbal communication and another box with dozens of examples of tone. Have each participant take one out of each box and act it out. You will find that the audience can pretty often guess the characteristics. Beyond that, sometimes they will be contradictory and other times they will be complementary. For example, they may get sloppy posture and bad eye contact combined with an enthusiastic, energetic tone with a fast cadence. Very confusing. On the opposite spectrum, one might draw a nice smile and professional demeanor combined with an articulate tone that is confident and soothing. In this case they complement each other.

But here is the kicker, the $64,000 question. When crisis communicators prepare their leadership for interviews, with talking points in hand (the words), how much time, if any, is spent providing guidance on nonverbals and tone? We addressed this briefly in Chapter six. Usually extraordinarily little. And if you are in the exceedingly small minority who addresses nonverbal and tone, how much time do you give it compared to the words? Be honest. And yet, if the statistics are even remotely close to accurate, the nonverbal and tone account for drastically more than the words. We might have our priorities bass ackwards. At a minimum, most crisis communications training and interview preparation could dedicate more time to these factors. At least 5% more. If we are willing to tell our boss what to say, we should also be willing to tell them respectfully that they slouch, have poor eye contact, and talk too fast. At the same time, it is a terrific opportunity to reinforce those nonverbals and tone they do well.

I would write more words, but it is always less about what we say than how we say it.

###

Chapter 12 The Reality of Artificial Intelligence

"Leaders and communicators must adapt to AI, but understanding how humans respond to messages is part of that journey."

-Bryn Travis, West Chester University, West Chester, PA.

"Nothing is so painful to the human mind as a great and sudden change."

-Mary Shelley, Frankenstein

Chapter 12   The Reality of Artificial
Intelligence by Rebecca Kuperberg

We hear about AI everywhere: personalized recommendations, chatbots, even self-driving cars. It seems like magic, but what is the real story behind it?

This chapter cuts through the hype and dives into the reality of AI. We will explore what it is, how it works, and what it means for our future.

Rather good, right? Everything in italics, above, was written by Bard, Google's AI (Artificial Intelligence) language application. If you are not familiar with Bard, you may have heard of ChatGPT, a similar application that was named the "fastest-growing consumer application in history."[50]

Users prompt ChatGPT for information and can ask for a response on a topic or theme, in a particular style, at a certain length, and with other specific requests. With additional filtering— "more humor!"—ChatGPT will continue to hone the message.

---

[50] ChatGPT sets record for fastest-growing user base - analyst note | Reuters

With the introduction above, I asked Bard to "give an introduction to a chapter titled 'The Reality of Artificial Intelligence.'" It spit out some convincing, but complex language: *Artificial intelligence (AI) has transitioned from a futuristic concept to a ubiquitous presence in our daily life.* I then prompted "using simpler language" to get the lines that started this chapter.

When I asked, "applied to emergency management," Bard responded: *In the midst of an emergency, every second counts. Fortunately, artificial intelligence (AI) is emerging as a powerful tool that can make a real difference in the lives of first responders and those affected by disasters.*

Honestly, I am a little annoyed. Bard continued with specific ways that AI can be a strength and a challenge, some of which were the very ideas that I had intended to explore in this chapter. These experiments remind me that AI can be useful and can help us be more efficient. I will share some emergency management-specific examples of AI's uses and efficiencies in this chapter. But we also have to approach AI with caution. Not only because it may be annoying to be outwritten by a machine, but because AI can do some considerable damage in the real world.

30,000 feet: What are we even talking about

Defining AI
Before we delve into whether AI is a villain or a hero, I want to take some time to define AI. According to the National Defense Authorization Act (2020), artificial intelligence refers to "a machine-based system that can, for a given set of human-defined objectives, make predictions, recommendations or decisions influencing real or virtual environments."

What does that mean? More simply, artificial intelligence refers to a machine automating tasks that a human would usually complete. This may sound like a scene from *The Matrix* or Tony Stark's assistant, J.A.R.V.I.S. in *Iron Man*. J.A.R.V.I.S. stands for "Just a Rather Very Intelligent System," another concise definition of artificial intelligence. But this is not just Jetsons-level science fiction. Many of us use artificial intelligence every day without even thinking about it.

Some examples of daily artificial intelligence include:

- Using Face ID to open our phones.
- Searching for an answer on Google.
- Searching for an answer on Google and the search bar "auto completing" our request, offering us common search phrases based on what we type.
- When Netflix recommends a show or movie based on what we have already watched.
- Asking Alexa to set a calendar reminder.
- Using grammar and spell check when drafting an email.
- Checking the traffic in Google Maps or Waze.
- Trying to reach Customer Service and finding yourself chatting with a computer instead.
- Your bank is sending you a fraud alert, asking if you were the one completing your recent purchase.

It is not just us as individuals; federal agencies use artificial intelligence as a key part of their work. The U.S. Postal Service (USPS), for example, uses AI to read addresses, determine postage costs, and track packages around the country.

The examples above appear harmless. And they usually are. AI makes our lives easier, creating efficiencies that we integrate into our routines. But not all AI is harmless. In the Russia-Ukraine war, deepfake videos—when the media is manipulated to make it appear that someone is saying something they are not—showed Ukrainian President Zelensky surrendering.[51] AI can also take images of any of us and turn them into fake pornography or show us saying vile things. It can be used to imitate our voices to terrify or defraud our loved ones. These darker sides of artificial intelligence are deeply concerning.

The increased attention to AI over the last few years is due to bigger systems with larger impacts. [52] In 2019 there were 123 tracked AI controversies. In 2021, there were 260.
AI is changing rapidly. That makes it harder to write laws and policies. It also makes it harder to even write or talk about AI. But just because it is

---

[51] Deepfake presidents used in Russia-Ukraine war (bbc.com)
[52] 2023 State of AI in 14 Charts (stanford.edu)

changing does not mean we can put our hands over our eyes and pretend it is not happening. AI is not going anywhere. If anything, it is getting better and faster, more easily replacing longer, tedious, and more expensive processes.

Artificial but not Autonomous

But it is also important to remember that AI is not independent, at least not yet. Humans program AI. AI learns from us- from the writing we have done, the posts we have made, the pictures we have taken, and the feedback we give. When my toddler asks Alexa or Siri for the "ABCs" and the system plays The Jackson 5, our feedback teaches Alexa that we mean "The Alphabet song," not just today, but on repeat for weeks and weeks on end.

Because AI learns from humans, it is also not without bias. If anything, it can amplify our biases. For example: Joy Buolamwini, founder of the Algorithmic Justice League, writes about how AI systems are more accurate when classifying the gender of male, light-skinned faces.[53] This

---

[53] Artificial Intelligence Has a Racial and Gender Bias Problem | TIME

has profound consequences for fields that rely on facial recognition technology like public safety.

In other studies, researchers found that robots were reproducing racist and sexist stereotypes because they were trained by popular artificial intelligence algorithms based on images and text created by people.

Automated decisions are not autonomous; they come from information that we all create and refine every day.

AI in Emergency Management

AI is already part of the emergency management landscape. It is a tool to improve outcomes for survivors and communities, as well as a threat.

The City of Portland, in Oregon, is testing using AI to handle non-emergency calls.[54] AI will help screen whether the caller needs information that AI can share directly or whether the caller should speak to a 311 operator. Moving more calls to the 311 system has helped reduce high call volumes to the city's emergency response 9-1-1 operators.

---

[54] City of Portland tests AI during non-emergency calls | kgw.com

Academic researchers expect that AI will play a more significant role in predicting weather and climate disasters in the future.[55] Recently, MIT researchers designed an AI-based program to help predict rare catastrophes, like bridge collapses.[56] They found that artificial intelligence is more accurate than traditional models at predicting rare, emergency events.[57]

But AI's influence on emergency management is not exclusively positive. In her remarks to the National Association of Emergency Managers (NEMA) in October 2023, FEMA Administrator Deanne Criswell described the "growing nexus between AI and scientific research" as an "increasing risk to public health.[58] Specifically, she noted a concern—shared by the members of Congress—that AI could help create harmful biochemical products like bioweapons or novel viruses. In this way, AI might be a major

---

[55] AI Should Predict More Weather and Climate Disasters in 2024 (northeastern.edu)
[56] MIT scientists design AI that could predict rare disasters - Big Think
[57] How machine learning could help forecast future disasters | World Economic Forum (weforum.org)
[58] FEMA Administrator Deanne Criswell's Remarks to the National Association of Emergency Managers | FEMA.gov

contributor to a future disaster. Artificial intelligence can also compromise our infrastructure, contributing to incidents now and in the future. Hospital systems and energy companies can be hacked more easily, putting lives at risk.

There are a few takeaways I would like to leave you with. First, we already use AI in our everyday lives and in our profession. And there is no turning back. Second, AI does not have to be something that you can only understand with a computer science degree. We may not be able to write code or adjust algorithms, but we can—and must—understand what AI does and how it impacts our work. Third, AI is not objective or perfect. And fourth, we must approach AI with caution.

Three Feet: Strategies to respond to change

One of the quotes that opens this chapter is from Mary Shelley's *Frankenstein.* That is appropriate. If AI is a monster, it is one we created for ourselves.

Shelley writes, "Nothing is so painful to the human mind as a great and sudden change." And while we can debate whether or not that's true, AI has changed our world while it is also changing at a rapid and unrelenting pace. This makes it hard to get a grasp on. This change can be frightening, especially for those who are already uncomfortable with technology. But ignoring AI will not make it go away. Instead, ignoring artificial intelligence could leave us and our communities vulnerable.

In thinking about how we manage and respond to AI, I can share specific tools or strategies, developed by people smarter than I am. But with the fast-changing pace of artificial intelligence, I worry that these tools will become out of date by the time you read them. Instead, I would like to encourage you to stay current on this fast-moving field, be proactive, and avoid the (AI) easy way.

Stay in the Know
Information about AI innovation is usually not written for a general audience. It is technical, often academic, and requires background knowledge. In short, it does not make sense and is off-putting. But it is also important that we stay informed of new and future changes to best protect ourselves and our communities. There are

a few resources that I find particularly helpful:

- The Conversation: this is a blog where academics write for broader audiences.
- Long-form journalism: For specific, concise updates about policies or tools, a regular article will suffice. But for a deeper understanding of what is changing and how it fits into a broader puzzle, I have found few better sources of information on AI than a well-written long-form piece in a newspaper or news magazine.
- Podcasts: There are a lot of podcasts that discuss technology. And as a casual podcast listener, I find it hard to weed through them all. Some recommended podcasts include Hard Fork, A.I. Nation, and Human vs. Machines.

Proactive, not Reactive

As a graduate student, I studied hate speech. Major social media companies use hate speech filters powered by AI. And though hate speech is still on social media platforms, AI-based filters help massively. These filters find and remove hate speech. As a bonus, they do not require content moderators—real human beings—to read horrible and horrifying online hate.

Initially, hate speech filters had a list of words they looked for. Classic hate speech. Words and phrases that are undeniably racist, sexist, etc. It was not perfect. Sometimes filtering for those words silenced people who were not being hateful, such as online users trying to expose hate speech or reclaim words to empower their communities. But it was a start.

However, technology and AI cannot (at least not yet) replace humans. Bad-faith internet actors looking to spread hate online are creative and they learned that their post would be removed, or their account blocked if they used hate speech. Let us imagine that "lilac" is a sexist word. Instead of writing "lilac" in their posts and risking a hate speech filter, users started writing "lil@c" or "1i1ac," getting the same point across but skirting around automated filters.

For a while, filters and the computer scientists who created them, were playing hate speech whack-a-mole. And to an extent, they still are. But just as bad actors got creative, so did those seeking to remove hate speech online. Engineers and computer scientists taught their artificial intelligence programs to incorporate different forms of hate speech creativity, some that existed and some that did not exist yet. They shifted from a reactive posture to a proactive one.

We should take this lesson as well. AI is changing and improving at an alarming rate. Legislation can take too long to write, pass, and implement in order to respond to this fast-changing landscape in specific ways. But only responding reactively leaves us playing whack-a-mole and never getting ahead of challenges. I do not oppose legislation. In fact, legislation is important in establishing enforceable guidelines and setting priorities. But in addition to slow-moving laws, flexible policies can help organizations account for quick change, establish broader priorities, and respond to the fast pace of technological change.

Avoid the easy way out
AI is efficient. It saves us time and energy. How much easier is it to open our phones by holding them up to our faces rather than type in a passcode?

But not all AI efficiencies are created equal. For example, I could have used ChatGPT or Bard to write this entire chapter. I promise, I did not. For three main reasons. First, despite giving me a fairly good outline, I had stories and personal knowledge that I wanted to share that ChatGPT just cannot predict. Second, there is a moral question here. If I put my name to a chapter, it is because I wrote it, not an online tool. And third, there are legal questions, many still being worked out. AI language processors, like ChatGPT, are pulling from existing sources. Should those sources get credit or be cited? If so, how?

Drafting an article, a blog post, or a social media post using AI *seems* easier. It is fast and mostly free. AI has a good grasp on English spelling and grammar, requiring less proofreading and oversight. But when we put information into AI programs, we lose control over that information and its security.

I will not suggest that you never use AI. Particularly in this fast-moving field, it is possible that in five years, we will all be using it in ways we cannot even imagine today. I also cannot speak to every emergency manager or every incident and challenge we will face.

But I can and should warn that private and secure information should not be uploaded to AI programs. Not yet. Being able to craft a great message in several seconds seems great. But spending months, years, trying to limit the spread of confidential information or regain security? Definitely not the easy way out.

Technology should work for us. We should continue to take advantage of the strengths of AI: detecting catastrophes, helping reach people with critical messages, and planning for future changes like rising sea levels. But while we take advantage of those strengths, we need to keep our eyes open to the challenges and dangers of AI.

I will leave you with some thoughts on the "artificial" aspect of artificial intelligence. Dan ends a blogpost on AI by writing the following: *Artificial Intelligence is not humanity. Let us protect ourselves and make sure it serves us without violating us.*[59]

In our best interactions with others, including our communications, we lead with our humanity. We

---

[59] Human-Adjacent is not Human - by Dan Stoneking (substack.com)

connect with disaster survivors and community members because of that humanity. It is one of the greatest strengths we bring to our work. AI can serve us, but we need to know when we should leave it behind and let our humanity take the lead.

###

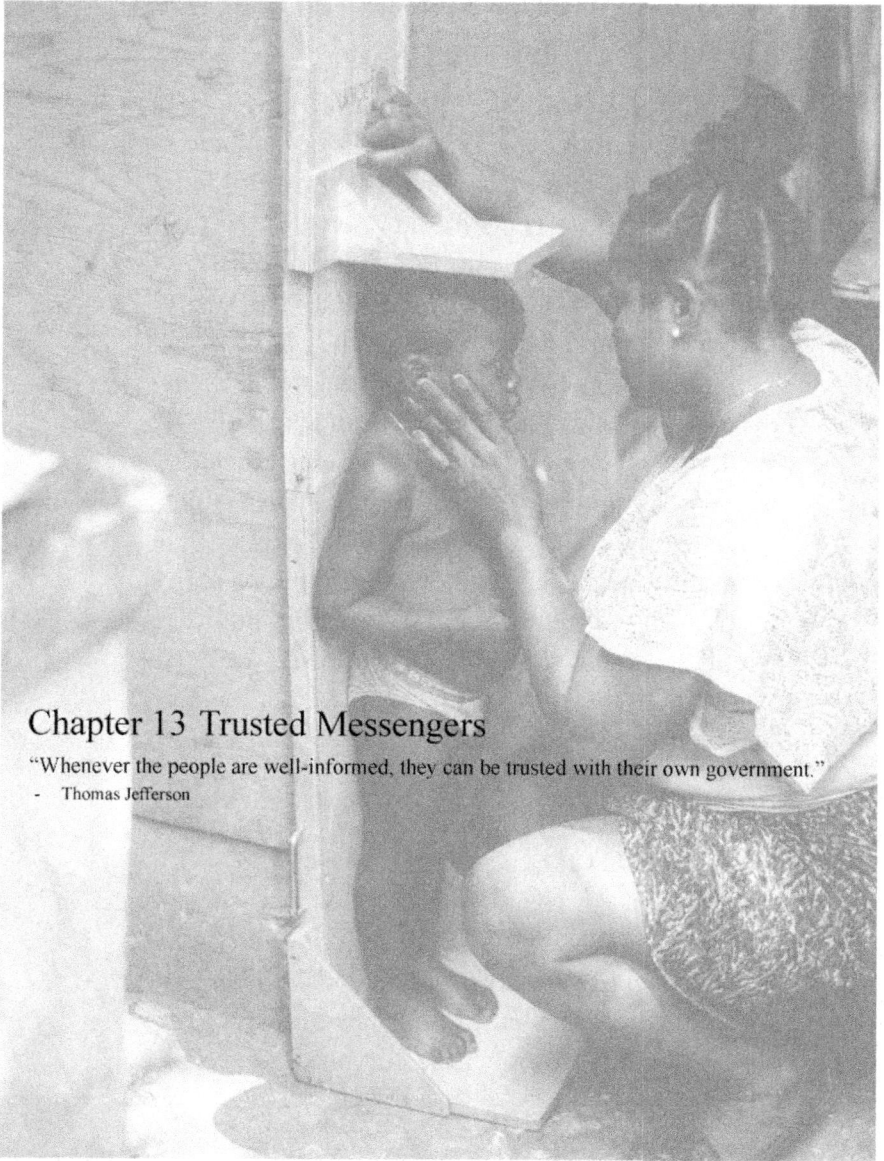

Chapter 13 Trusted Messengers

"Whenever the people are well-informed, they can be trusted with their own government."

- Thomas Jefferson

Chapter 13   Trusted Messengers By Dan
Stoneking

The Children's Nutrition Program of Haiti
(CNP/Kore Timoun) is a non-profit organization
working to raise a generation of healthy children
who can then raise Haiti from poverty. As of this
writing, they have helped more than 10,000
families and 93% of their staff are Haitian, many
of whom live in the communities they serve.[60]
There are groups like this across the globe. Some
are for profit, some non-profit. Some are faith-
based, others are not. Some of them are elected
officials, though most are not. They differ on the
help and services they provide to make their
community better. But the one thing that so many
groups who work in, of, and for the communities
have in common is that they are trusted. We need
to work with these trusted partners and embrace
them as trusted messengers.

30,000 Feet

During the COVID vaccination phase,
Philadelphia, PA established the Center City
Vaccination Center (CCVC). Initially, there was
a broad level of skepticism and distrust. The
CCVC partners implemented trusted messenger
tours. This program leveraged community

---

[60] Kore Timoun

leaders, elected officials, and other credible voices as trusted messengers. The federally supported vaccination mission in Philadelphia found many advocates to inform and impact communities that would not have been reached through other channels.[61] The CCVC conducted more than thirty trusted messenger tours and engagement events with various community-based organizations and faith-based organizations representing a diverse array of the City's population. Each tour highlighted the federally supported site's language interpretation capabilities (which included a dozen on-site interpreters in at least six languages), one hundred wheelchairs, access and functional need considerations, introductions to the site's Civil Rights and Disability Integration staff, and an overview of the vaccination process itself.

At the same time, the Livingston County, IL, Health Department also "identified highly trusted community members, including local physicians and religious leaders, as key messengers in disseminating accurate information about the safety and effectiveness of COVID-19 vaccines."[62]

---

[61] *Philadelphia Vaccine Mission,* Outreach Final Report
[62] *A Strategy to Tackle Public Health Information,* American Hospital Association

Trusted messengers existed before COVID, but the fear of vaccines significantly increased the value of this tool. In 2022, the Ad Council Research Institute conducted a Trusted Messenger study and summarized four key data points as follows.[63]

- *"The closer a messenger is to a person, the more they trust them in later stages of the knowledge journey.*
- *Younger Americans—especially Gen Z— are more likely to trust social media influencers and celebrities across all stages of the knowledge journey.*
- *Trust in scientists, professionals and academics remains very low among Republicans.*
- *Americans in urban areas are much more trusting overall than those in other areas."*

That is just one study and limited in scope. But it does highlight the complexity of trusted messenger programs. Furthermore, every crisis is different. The trusted messengers for vaccinations will not be the same ones during a nuclear power plant accident. Trusted messengers

---

[63] *2022 Trusted Messenger Survey,* Ad Council Research Institute

can be a valuable force multiplier, but they do not come without challenges.

Three Feet

Finding trusted messengers during a crisis is possible, but not ideal. Crisis communicators are well served to get to know as many potential trusted messenger groups as possible before the next disaster. This includes building a database, distribution group, and building relationships with groups like the following:

- Non-profits
- Associations
- Faith-based
- Local elected officials
- Law Enforcement
- Fire and Rescue
- Medical Services
- Local Celebrities
- Small businesses
- Hotel/Lodging
- Trade Unions
- Academia
- Hospitality
- Residential Services
- Influencer

As you develop and consider these relationships, understand that separate groups may be helpful during different crises and that relationships continue to change. Get to know their reputations in the community, their perceived level of integrity, and empathy. For example, Law Enforcement typically are more supported and trusted in rural areas than big cities. Some celebrities are adored by most, while others have a specific audience. It is also helpful to understand the level of access you have to the group as well as the level of access the group has to the community or portions thereof. What amount of influence do they have? You will need to decide, and constantly reevaluate who delivers the message.

Trusted messengers are not without risk. Therefore, for each group identify the pros and cons. Common pros may include that certain groups have more credibility than yours in different communities and/or on different topics. Also, a trusted messenger typically has the latitude to say things that your organization cannot. In addition, as you increase trusted messengers, you build coalitions. More voices reach more audiences. If some members of the community trust group A and others trust group B, but both groups are saying and reinforcing your messages, you just effectively reached more people.

But keep your eyes on the cons. Your reputation becomes linked with your trusted messenger.

Research your potential messengers online, in the media, and through the community. Another con is that some of these groups may be trusted and trustworthy, but they may not fully understand your objectives and your message. It is essential to ensure they fully understand. An ideal trusted partner is one who understands the topic and is respected in the topic even more than your organization. After a relationship is merged, keep in mind that relationships and priorities change. Stay tuned in and be prepared to move on once the relationship is either not mutually beneficial or fails to be effective.

The last area to consider is the implementation of these relationships. It starts by simply building a database. This should be followed by personal engagement to include attending their meetings and events where possible. As you prepare to engage in partnership on a specific topic, it can be as simple as sharing your talking points and messages for them to use. I personally used this form of trusted messenger for an entire hurricane season with a national correspondent for CNN. I quickly learned that he believed in me and our organization and was loyal to accurately reporting our work. Eventually, I started taking my talking points and simply deleted the "Talking Point" heading and sent the bullets to him as an "update." Each night, I would hear my words come out of his mouth on national television. He was respected as a retired military spokesperson. The relationship benefited us both.

A deeper commitment to trusted messengers is to provide them a tour of the event, work, or facility of the current crisis and give them total freedom to report and share with their constituents in their own words. There is a greater risk here (trust), but also a bigger win since their sincerity will always be more impactful than simply repeating key messages.

At this point you may be thinking, sure, sounds good, but I do not have the time or the resources. Well, the databases can be created by either an administrative assistant or part-time help. The outreach can overlap with your normal outreach anyway. Take a look at the workload of each member of your team. There is always one who can take on an additional duty. Finally, it is a simple matter of cost-benefit, or as I prefer, "bang for the buck." Is it worth twenty hours of staff time spread over a few months to have more voices, highly respected individuals, telling your story effectively?

Can you afford not to do it?

###

Chapter 14 Stakeholder Engagement

"I enjoy mixed audiences, not one particular group. Short, tall, scientists, Jews, gentiles, whatever, as long as they breathe and like to laugh."

- Don Dickles

"If civilization is to survive, we must cultivate the science of human relationships - the ability of all peoples, of all kinds, to live together, in the same world at peace."

- Frankline D. Roosevelt.

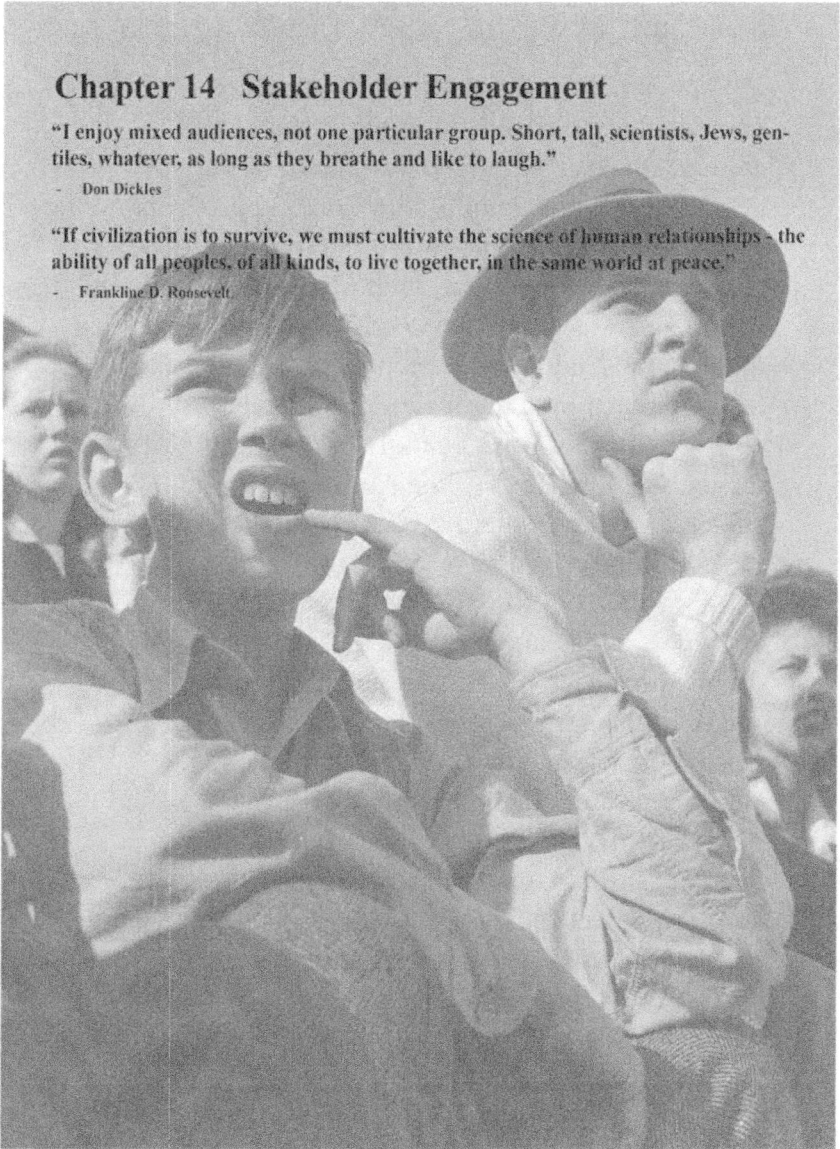

Chapter 14   Stakeholder Engagement by Dan Stoneking

In September, 2009, I deployed to American Samoa after the islands were struck by two earthquakes that generated a tsunami, killing nearly 200 people, annihilating some villages and causing more than \$200 million in damages.[64] A few days after my arrival, in the quiet bay of Pago Pago, surrounded by Pacific hills that reach to the clouds, nestled between Sadie's by the Sea restaurant and the Pago Pago Yacht Club, just next to Samoana High School, I was working in the unassuming Rex H. Lee Auditorium. The students would saunter by wearing their light blue traditional lava lava school uniforms. Lunch goers strolled out from a satisfying midday meal at Sadie's and island buses picked-up and dropped-off customers at the Yacht Club bus stand, exchanging pleasantries. The yacht club was unique, to me, in its charm as it had no yachts but rather lined the shore with island outrigger canoes. In the middle of the gentle bustle of the day, on any other day, the auditorium would boast local dances and concerts, where the songs would echo out the bay.

---

[64] *"2009 Samoa Islands Tsunami,"* NOAA

But it was not any other day. That day, the auditorium had been converted to a Disaster Recovery Center. They came together out of necessity. They came together to recover. It quickly became clear to me that they were extremely family oriented. Their islands were made up of villages, each led by a Chief, or Matai. One evening, a few days later, one of the Chiefs invited us to his village to explain recovery options to the villagers. Before we began, the young children of the village sang songs for us. There were only about thirty-five people in attendance that night, but they hung on our every word and treated us with such kindness and gratitude. It was a strong reminder to me that every community is different. Every engagement is different.

In early January 2010, I deployed to Haiti to help people respond and recover from the devastating earthquake that killed more than 200,000 people.[65] I remember sitting in the U.S. Embassy one morning in Port-au-Prince, Haiti. Many ceiling tiles were missing or hanging down, with lights and cables dangling among them. The paintings on the walls were cracked, broken or askew. And each cubicle was littered with files and folders that scattered upon the earthquake's

---

[65] *"Haiti Earthquake 2010,"* Internet Geography

impact. While I was getting ready for another long day, I noticed a quote, written across a background photograph of a Mapou tree, "Life to me is like a tree, if it doesn't take its time to bloom during spring, it'll be too late in fall… there will only be the trunk and the branches left.…" – Dominique M. H. Franck Jean, 1992

Haiti forests are disappearing at an enormous rate each year. The Haitians are investing in their trees. And during this recovery, they were investing in themselves, as well. On that particular morning I tagged along to a meeting about cluster group coordination. There were quite a few different stakeholders represented in the meeting, including non-profits, faith-based, companies, and government agencies. They each led a different *cluster*, or responsible function, hence the name. I had no role in the meeting. As a communicator, I just sat in the back to gain a better understanding of all the responsibilities and capabilities so I could be more empowered to tell their stories.

About thirty different people spoke, one after another, briefing out, representing their organizations. It was still early in the response phase. There was no back and forth dialogue, simply a quick status update and then on to the next. The 12th speaker briefed that they had a handful of trucks and where they were, but as of yet, they did not have any cargo. Around twenty minutes later the 26th speaker shared that they had some food and medical supplies, but no way to transport them. I immediately sat up straighter in my chair, seeing the opportunity for a good news story. But they just moved on to the 27th briefer. When all were done, the gentlemen in charge thanked them for their briefings and reminded them to all return tomorrow, same time, same place. I was worried about cultural sensitivities, but even more worried that survivors might miss much needed help, so I interrupted and asked if I could speak before they closed out. I verified that one of them had transportation without cargo and the other had cargo without transportation and suggested that they could work together. Fortunately, they appreciated my catch and did, in fact, collaborate to move the supplies that very day to where they were needed.

In that moment, I was reminded that every stakeholder brings something different to the table, we all have needs and capabilities, and that success depends on meaningful two-way dialogues.

30,000 Feet

Upon my return from Haiti, I transitioned to a new role as the Director, Private Sector, within the Office of External Affairs at FEMA. I am often asked the what and why of FEMA having External Affairs instead of Public Affairs, like most agencies, organizations and corporations. I like to answer because I think it is an outstanding model. External Affairs at FEMA includes Public Affairs, Congressional Affairs, Intergovernmental Affairs, Private Sector Outreach, Tribal Engagement, Preparedness Communications, and Disability Integration. The beauty and value is that by working together within the same structure, we are better synchronized, better informed, and we have gained an appreciation for the nuances to stakeholder engagement.

Private sector engagement was a new experience for me. It sounded interesting and I was eager to explore. But I also must admit that on my first day there, I could not even imagine the breadth and depth of engagement and endless possibilities, simply by reaching out to share needs and capabilities in ongoing conversations with the private sector.

Working hand-in-hand with the private sector, we hosted the first-in-nation conference on "Building Resilience through Public-Private Partnerships." I saw in 2023 that this event celebrated its 12th straight year. We created the National Business Emergency Operation Center, and it all started with a sketch on a napkin when a few of us went out to lunch. We began a 90-day rotation bringing individual private actor leaders to work inside FEMA to advise and collaborate. We created and filled private sector liaison positions in all ten of our regions. We created a public-private partnership web-based training course. We increased our national level exercise from sixty-five private sector partners to more than 3,000. We did all of that and so much more in less than eighteen months, all because of stakeholder engagement.

As a result of that investment in this stakeholder group and understanding each other's needs and capabilities through constant two-way communication, we were able to help survivors in countless ways. We worked with the Outdoor Advertising Association of America to post countless survivor-centric messages on electronic billboards across the nation through a multitude of disasters. We were able to work with Lowes to bring much needed refrigeration units into Joplin, MO after a tragic tornado to store units of blood. We partnered with Walgreens to ensure the stores they shipped restock to in New England in the middle of a disaster were the same stores that would have power to support them. We joined with WWE, NFL, MLB, and NASCAR to get disaster assistance information to attendees at sporting events in or near communities impacted by a disaster. We even collaborated with the Goodyear Blimp to drive donations to disaster-plagued communities. There was more. Much more.

The point of all of this is to reinforce how much can be accomplished through a commitment to stakeholder engagement.

Three Feet

Marketing and outreach to the elderly has fascinated me for some time. Moreso, now that I am considered elderly. I think. Ages are strange. When we are young, the movie theaters tell us we are adults at 12 years old. Then we are told we can fight and die for our country at 18 and we can vote then as well. But often we cannot have that first (legal) alcoholic drink until we are 21 years old.

The same inconsistencies occur on the other end. The American Association of Retired Persons (AARP) sent me an unsolicited membership card on my 50th birthday. No gift, but the card was a nice gesture, even if I was not retired yet. And by the way, if AARP has the ability to find all of us the very second that we turn fifty, we are underestimating their skills. They could have found Bin Laden much faster. Then, Denny's restaurant started offering me senior meals when

I turned fifty-five. I still prefer a little more spice in my food, but it felt nice that I had achieved another plateau. Turning sixty, my body told me that I am old. Primarily, the knees and the back. At 62, I just retired. That sure seems like a sign. And now sixty-five is not too far off. I am going to have to figure out that whole Medicare thing. So, I am in the ballpark of being a senior or elderly or whatever we want to call ourselves.

And it has me thinking – if it is so hard to figure out when we become adults and later when we become seniors, then it must be harder still to figure out how to market to us. I do not think I have much in common with folks in their late eighty's. I am not sure if I even know anyone in their late eighty's. And while I am retired at 62, I have a different outlook and consume information a bit different from someone still working, even if they are in their mid-seventies.

We get defined, packaged, and labeled in so many ways. Age. Gender. Race. Religion. Politics. I recently bought a kayak. I would rather that marketers label me and reach out to me as a kayaker. A few weeks ago, I made the mistake of searching for comfortable socks on the internet. Now my social media feeds are filled with ads for socks for seniors. Targeted internet advertising. Ugh. On the other side, I recently also clicked on a picture of Salma Hayek in a bikini. Since then, I have been inundated. Not all targeting is bad.

I actually learned that I am in a specific sub-category for seniors – the socially active retirees. I saw a marketing plan for us that said we like throw blankets, watches, golf, and personalized coffee mugs. Um. No, no, no, and no.

In all honesty, my fascination has more to do with me becoming a senior than how anyone wants to market to me. And I am an anomaly or a glitch. I am not ready for adult diapers and meals on wheels. So, if you do not mind, just think of me as a kayaker. And if you have to get me a personalized mug, please make sure it has a picture of Salma Hayek in a bikini on it. The broader point here, from the other side, is to recognize the complexities and nuances of each stakeholder group.

My reflections here gave me an appreciation for stakeholder outreach on the stakeholder side of the fence. There are things you can do today to begin building a coalition of stakeholders.

- *Value Proposition.* You may only have a few stakeholders. You may only have the media. You may have plenty. You can always have more. The world is large, so you may need to prioritize. As you grow, you may need to convince your leadership and the stakeholder on the value of building a relationship. Your leadership needs to know that the relationship will help the organization achieve its mission and vision. They will want assurances that the relationship will not impact organizational reputation. Oftentimes, stakeholders are simpler. Why? What is in it for me? That varies depending on your organization but must be clear. Justifications can include enhanced access, information sharing, or a temporary seat at your table. There could be economic benefits or philanthropic benefits. Make sure you know which stakeholders you want and why they would want to engage with you.

- *Identification.* Determining where you might increase your coalition begins with brainstorming. A trivia team can answer more questions correctly than an individual. This step is a suitable time to prioritize. Maybe focus on academia this year and faith-based next year. Older Americans this year, younger ones the next.
- *Divide and Conquer.* Unless you are a one-person shop, you have an opportunity to divide and conquer the workload. It also creates advocates. If a member of

your team has the lead for access and functional needs engagement, then every time that person is in a meeting or reviewing a plan, they will instinctively think of the impacts to their stakeholders. From the stakeholder side they will appreciate having a champion they can contact.

- **Distribution.** This is not sexy or necessarily fun (for most of us). But sometimes you have to do foundational work to set yourself up for success. Let us say you have decided to add firefighters in the state of Maryland to your stakeholders. Create a distribution that includes every fire station, county fire officials, state fire officials, fire associations, and other connections that may relate. Try to include name, title, phone, email, and address (you never know which will come in handy). If they have generic email addresses, include those too. For example, both fred.jones@bethesda.md as well as firechief@bethesda.md both make sense so you still have a connection to the new fire chief when Fred retires. Congratulations Fred. Remember, this skill of research and typing is administrative. Anyone can do it. Part-time help. Friend. Convince the boss to get other parts of the organization to help for a few weeks.

- **Posture.** Whether working with the media or any other stakeholder, we need to determine the right posture. When I first began working as a spokesperson, the posture was simple, and like a light switch. We were either on (active and engaging) or off (passive and silent). Over time, the profession got a bit more sophisticated and realized that engagement is more like a dimmer switch, as circumstances unfold, we may need to become a little more active or a little more passive and be flexible enough to adjust slightly in either direction. In our complex world today, especially during a crisis, with constantly changing information and a bevy of stakeholders, we have learned to manage our posture more like an equalizer in a sound recording studio. The sound engineer knows that sometimes they must turn the Low Mid Frequency knob up to provide more warmth and the High Frequency knob down to reduce brightness. In stakeholder engagement, think of the knobs as the different stakeholders. They need different things at separate times.

The media may want a soundbite. Congressional members may need a detailed briefing. Private sector partners need to know how to help. Know your stakeholders and keep adjusting, as necessary.

- **Outreach.** The first time you reach out to the group, by email, needs to be an upbeat, compelling pitch. Let them know that you have created this stakeholder group and would like to be able to email them with updates and opportunities about once a month. Assure them that they will not be overwhelmed, but rather you want a mutually beneficial relationship. Use the value proposition you created. Whenever you email them, always offer something first. Then if you have a reasonable ask, you can segue to that. Try not to end any correspondence without offering them to produce other ideas, suggestions or recommendations. Whether you are corporate or government, overcome all of your instincts and do not write like a bureaucrat. If you write, "Good morning, on behalf of Director Jones, I would like to introduce you to our mission statement here at Widgets International…," your email will be deleted. Try something like this instead, "Hi, my daughter Chloe told me yesterday that she wants to be a firefighter when she grows up. She said, 'firefighters are cool," and I agree. So, I am hoping you would like to do some cool things on the planet together that will be low-effort and high-reward…."

- *Engagement.* So now, you are talking. You are engaging, well sort of engaging. This is where most people who try to do outreach fail. They fall into a monthly update, or worse yet, a bulletin (less people open attachments than read the email). The writing becomes bureaucratic and pedantic. So, do not be that person. Make every outreach meaningful. be innovative and creative. Invite them to exercise, physical or virtual. Offer three to five ways you think your organizations can collaborate and then bend to their preferences as long as they are beneficial. Give them credit and recognition for their efforts through   social media and other platforms. Be cool. Convince them to be an active member of the cool kids club.
- *Survivors.* Some people consider survivors and those impacted by a crisis as a stakeholder group. I do not. It is semantics. But survivors are special, important, and paramount. We do not call

them 'victims,' because that is belittling. Simply, and consistently, referring to them as survivors and using their names and humanity is uplifting. And when you have your hand on the sound recording equalizer knob, always push it towards empathy and compassion.

- ***Internal.*** Every skill I have ever learned and applied in crisis communications work effectively with internal audiences as well. Heck, they have even helped me in personal relationships on more than a few occasions. As you interact with your team, your peers, and your leadership, many of these same engagement techniques work. And you do need to engage each of these groups. The value proposition is professional success.

###

Chapter 15 Historically Underserved Communities

"The hallmark of a healthy society has always been measured by how it cares for the disadvantaged."
- Joni Eareckson Tada

Chapter 15   Historically Underserved
Communities by Rebecca Kuperberg

According to a widely shared story, Margaret
Mead was once asked: what is the first sign of
civilization? Mead was a famous anthropologist
whose life's work was observing and studying
cultures around the world. She answered: a
15,000-year-old femur with a healed fracture. A
broken femur leaves a person unable to hunt,
collect water, or outrun predators without
assistance. A *healed* femur suggests that
someone was supported and cared for by others.
This is the measure of an advanced humankind.

We still have work to do. Yes, a broken femur is
survivable today. But our society often turns
away those who are struggling rather than
offering them the support they need. Entire
groups and communities are underserved.

Disasters often exacerbate these vulnerabilities.
Older adults, people with disabilities, the poor,
those in rural areas, and individuals who are
subject to discrimination face more challenges
during and following disasters.

Yes, we want all members of our community,
including those who are members of currently or

historically underserved groups, to survive incidents. But our goals should be more than just surviving. How can we ensure that all members of our community will not just survive, but thrive through recovery?

30,000 Feet: Equity is not just a buzzword

The Power of Words
What do we mean by historically underserved communities? And who has underserved them? Historically underserved refers to groups who have been subject to discrimination by Federal policies and programs.

Why not just say "minorities" or use another word? There are a number of categories that overlap with historically underserved groups, such as marginalized groups. Marginalized groups are those who are excluded from mainstream society and/or face discrimination from members of society. Many groups have been underserved by Federal policies *and* discriminated against. But these are not exactly the same. I will, however, use both of these terms in this chapter.

Both "marginalized" and "underserved" are different from "minorities" because marginalized and underserved put emphasize the society and policies doing the marginalizing. Some see terms like "minority" as too vague; redheads are a minority group! An alternative, *minoritized*, refers to the action, the process by which a group receives unequal treatment or is made into a minority.

The words we use to describe specific, historically underserved communities also matters. For those who are not active members in an underserved community, it can be frustrating or challenging that names can change over time, that some names are no longer acceptable to use, or that different people within a community may have different preferences. For example, in the U.S., *Black* is usually the preferred term over *African American*, though some individuals feel differently! I know I have struggled with not wanting to be wrong but also not wanting to ask for fear of appearing ignorant. Some also push back at this discomfort by labeling it "politically correct" to use some terms over others.

There are a few things I keep in mind. First, historically marginalized groups may push back on a name that was put *on* them and instead, prefer a name of their choosing. They may also want to reclaim a name, such as American Indian communities. Second, names change as times change. The gay or queer community has opened up to many more groups, some of which did not have formal names until recently, leading to the present-day LGBTQIA+ community. Finally, it is not right to assume that all members of a community feel and think exactly the same. People are different and are comfortable with different labels. When in doubt, ask!

Equity vs. Equality

The federal government has a legal obligation to act in an "equitable and impartial manner without discrimination on the grounds of race, color, religion, national origin, sex, age, disability, English proficiency, or economic status."[66] Many states have laws with similar requirements. We also have a moral responsibility to do what we can to push for equal outcomes prior to and following emergencies. But that ideal is not always reached and has not been fully achieved in our country's past. Generations of

---

[66] Office of Equal Rights | FEMA.gov

discriminatory policies have had impacts that reverberate into the present and include persistent poverty, mistrust of the federal government, and trauma.

To combat these histories, as well as marginalization that exists today, we push for equity. Equity, though similar in sound to equality, is different. Equality means that everyone gets the same resources, while equity gives different resources to people based on their dissimilar needs.

Let us use bicycles as an example. An equality approach would give a 4-year-old, someone in a wheelchair, and a cyclist the same bicycle. An equity approach gives a 4-year-old a bike with training wheels, a wheelchair user an adaptive bicycle, and a cyclist an adult bicycle. Will the 4-year-old end up winning a race against a cyclist? Not necessarily. But this example is about giving each individual the resources that make the most sense for them.

In emergency management, equity can be a goal for communicating during all parts of the disaster cycle. Over half of U.S. adults read at a sixth grade reading level or below.[67] In preparing community messages, using plain and accessible language means that all community members can understand the information. Not all community members can understand English. Translating important messages means that those with low English proficiency receive important emergency alerts. Having live interpretation at press conferences and events post-disaster enables Deaf and Hard of Hearing people to understand information about assistance that may otherwise be missed or misinterpreted. These are just a few examples of communicating with equity in mind, considering the unique needs of historically underserved groups.

Not Just Woke

Equity, diversity, and inclusion are used so frequently these days that they sometimes mean nothing at all. The use of these words has also prompted a backlash, saying that an emphasis on diversity or equity is "woke," just "politically correct," or taking time and resources away from issues that "really matter." I would like to push back on that.

---

[67] Do More Than Half of Americans Read Below 6th-Grade Level? | Snopes.com

Equity is not just about the "Oppression Olympics," a term you may be familiar with. The concept suggests that you can tally up someone's identities (race, gender, disability, class, sexuality, etc.) to determine who is most oppressed. Those who are most oppressed are seen as more authentic or their views more legitimate. Of course, our identities are not separable and scorable from most to least oppressed. I cannot separate out my experience as a woman and as an American, giving a percentage or a score to each; I am an American woman and my experience as a woman is informed by living in the U.S. and vice versa. Equity is about identifying how we can best serve all groups, recognizing how groups intersect and taking differences into account.

Advancing equity is also not about helping some disadvantaged groups over others. As activists have pointed out, when you are used to privilege, equality can feel like oppression. But pushing for equity should not be seen as cutting the pie into smaller and smaller pieces. Instead, in striving for equity we are making a bigger pie to give more to everyone. For example, nothing is lost by using plain language. Instead, those who previously could not understand may now be able. And those who could understand before, may understand better or faster now than they could previously! It is a win-win.

Equity also serves groups such as older and rural individuals. If we are lucky, we will get to be older adults. This is not a group that anyone is born into and may not be a historically underserved group in the way we imagine. But, in a disaster context, older adults have unique vulnerabilities. Older adults with disabilities may not be able to drive or may need caregiver support. Older adults may also have caring responsibilities for children, grandchildren, pets, partners, parents, and others that make evacuating or sheltering more challenging.

Individuals who live in rural areas—about one in five Americans according to the U.S. Census[68]-- may have limited cell service or internet that makes accessing information more difficult, especially in an emergency with disruptions to power and telecommunications. They may need to drive much further to access support, including shelter, or wait longer for emergency services.

---

[68] What is Rural America? (census.gov)

These challenges need to be addressed before disasters, in planning, as well as during and after disasters.

I do not believe that equity is just a buzzword. But I do believe that it is not always clear how to "do" equity. In the next section, I address a few ways to operationalize equity, to put equity into practice.

Three Feet: Operationalizing equity

Nothing about them, without them
In graduate school, I got a grant to study politics in Africa. I could go to any country I wanted and spend my time how I wanted, so long as it was on the continent of Africa and furthering my research. For the first part of my trip, I went to Ethiopia and Kenya. I wrote and presented a paper comparing both countries and how counter-terrorism efforts have been used to push back democratic rights.

After I presented my paper, I was introduced to a professor who had worked on Ethiopian women's movements for decades. After she congratulated me on my paper, I said, "Well you are the expert!" She responded, "No, the Ethiopian people are the experts." I was humbled by her response, and I think about it often.

None of us are experts in most people's lives. It would not be practical to go through every historically underserved group and offer suggestions for specific programs or policies that would help achieve equity with that group in mind. It is also not appropriate to assume that I, or anyone else, can speak to every group's experience.

Instead, the best way to help meet the needs of groups, particularly those that are marginalized or historically underserved, is to include them in the conversation. Trust people to know what they need to succeed. This means bringing them into the discussion from the start, not just including them for the "equity portion" or at the end of a process.

Getting information

How do we even know who is underserved? Or what groups require special services in disaster settings? One of the first steps is knowing our community.

Data, including census data in the U.S., can be a tremendous help. For example, LEP.gov has data on Limited English Proficiency communities across the U.S. with the ability to drill down to the county level. Other tools have information about age, religion, or class using other data like tax records, government benefits, and more. But these tools are not always up-to-date, accessible, or easy to understand.

The message and the messenger matters

People who work in and serve their communities are also an important source of information. They can offer richer data than simply a percentage. Community leaders can serve as trusted messengers who can share information that will not only be understood but trusted. They can understand the unique needs of the community within their community.

Other information changes how we interact with a community respectfully. By learning about the customs and practices of a group, we can incorporate these norms into what we communicate and how we communicate.

For example, observant Jewish communities do not use electricity on Saturday, the Sabbath (though, notably, there are exceptions for saving lives). They will not be able to access information transmitted electronically from sundown on Friday to dusk on Saturday. In towns or counties with large populations of observant Jews, alternative plans to share emergency alerts during the Sabbath need to be in place. Developing these plans in advance is not only practical but shows respect for the community.

Do not wait to be asked
It makes sense for us to imagine that groups, communities, and individuals will ask for what they need. If, as I just said, every group has beliefs and practices that inform how they receive information, shouldn't they share that information with us?

Here is where it matters that these are not merely groups but marginalized and/or historically underserved groups. Trust has been lost over time. In some cases, this is due to centuries of failed policies as well as exclusion and discrimination. We cannot assume that all groups will want to, or feel comfortable, asking for what they need.

Instead, by offering necessary services, we can invite people in. Rather than wait for Deaf and Hard of Hearing community members to come forward and ask for interpreters at press conferences and in Disaster Recovery Centers, they should be there. We are more likely to have communities show up when we show them that we care about their inclusion.

But also, ask questions

Just because we should not wait for groups to voice their needs, does not mean that we should only rely on our assumptions. There is some disagreement here. Some people feel that it is inappropriate to ask someone to teach us about their culture or preferences. Those from marginalized backgrounds should not be given yet another task. But this is not a fixed rule. It is also up to the individual. If you have close colleagues, friends, and family from other cultures or historically underrepresented groups, a well-meaning question will be welcome.

We can also learn by joining special emphasis or special interest groups, by doing research, and by seeking out training and classes. We can find spaces that are no-fault environments, where questions are encouraged. In these spaces, we can all learn from each other.

Learning from mistakes

In the wake of Typhoon Merbok, which hit Alaska's west coast in September 2022, FEMA hired a company in California to translate information about applying for assistance into two Alaska Native languages.[69] The translations made no sense. The issue was not just a waste of federal dollars. Survivors could not access necessary information and furthermore, the mistranslations—which were nonsense at best and incomprehensible at worst—were offensive to communities whose languages have historically been undervalued. The contracting company was fired, and FEMA made immediate corrections to the materials.[70] The agency also wrote guidance to prevent this from happening again.

This was a big mistake. And is not excusable. But I share it here both because it applies to this

---

[69] FEMA sent 'unintelligible' disaster relief information to Alaska Native people impacted by Typhoon Merbok - Alaska Public Media
[70] FEMA fires group for nonsensical Alaska Native translations | AP News

chapter and to note that mistakes can and do happen. We may mispronounce something or not realize that we are not following respectful protocols. As Maya Angelou said, "when you know better, do better." We cannot let mistakes in the past paralyze us. Instead, they can push us to do better now and in the future.

Many of us learned the Golden Rule in kindergarten: treat others as you want to be treated. This is a great start. But moving towards equity asks us to update our thinking and follow the Platinum Rule: treat others as *they* want to be treated. We do not all share the same traditions, priorities, or beliefs. But when it comes to emergency management, we all deserve to survive disasters and thrive in recovery. Helping all members of our society to thrive asks us, yes, to be kind but also to show respect, include others, and be open to learning and growing.

###

Blossoms

When the blossoms finally come, they can either wilt or be the cream of the crop. Others may never see or think about the seeding, growth, sun, shading, watering, placement, fertilizing, pruning, trimming, and effort that came before. And yet, these flowers and fruits are the magic, the pure, refined beauty of the gardener's creation. The gardener need not even reveal the secrets of the labor but can rather bask in the pleasure of the outcome. In this part, we will reveal ideas and opportunities that may seem esoteric and intangible, and yet they are the keys to growing a small nursery into a highly regarded botanical garden. These are the chapters that will become the tools that ensure you and your program stand out.

Chapter 16 Essential Human Characterisitics

"I have a dream that my four little children will one day live in a nation where they will not be judged by the color of their skin, but by the content of their character."

- Martin Luther King, Jr.

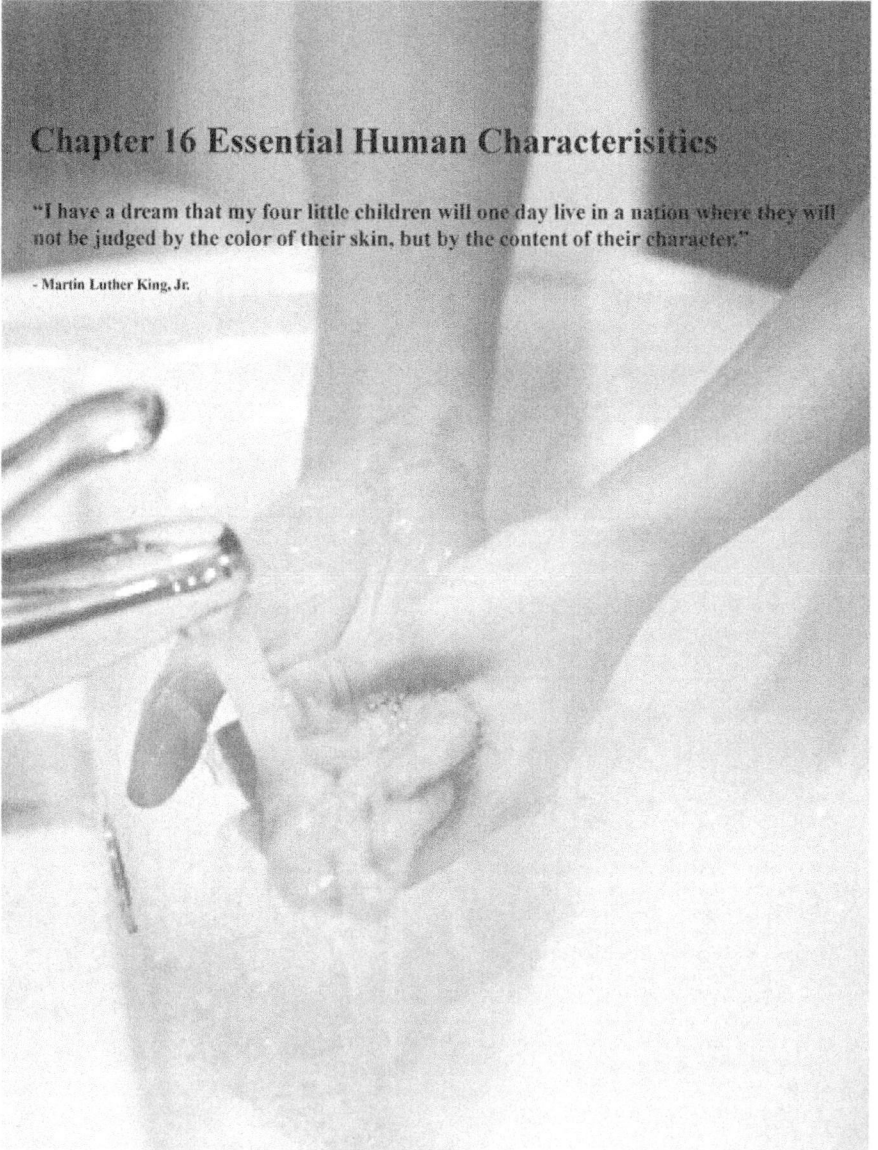

Chapter 16   Essential Human Characteristics
by Dan Stoneking

I have met and worked with all types of people in crisis communication positions. Some of them have been narcissists, sycophants, ethnocentric, verbose, and self-indulgent. Those are not preferred characteristics for this profession. The successful communicators I have met have been strategic, tactical, technically competent, human resource-oriented, logistic, selfless, message-focused warriors. That is the awesome sauce right there. The next few chapters will take a deeper dive into essential characteristics for success. Stories, experiences, and reflection help.

While I was in college, I skipped classes, drank beer, and went to parties. I joined a fraternity. While rushing a fraternity, we had to memorize a poem, "The True Gentlemen," by John Walter Wayland. I'm glad we memorized it. Because it took time to sink in while I was pushing boundaries and testing limits for the first time in my life.   In time, the poem began to shape who I would want to become, a model I still strive towards. Years later, as a teacher, I required my students to memorize it. I share it here in its entirety because, like Martin Luther King's speech, "I Have a Dream," it speaks to the very characteristics that every communicator should embody.

The True Gentleman is
The man whose conduct proceeds
from goodwill and an acute sense of
propriety, and whose self-control is
equal to all emergencies;
Who does not
make the
poor man conscious of his
poverty,
the obscure
man of his obscurity,
or any man
of his inferiority or
deformity;
Who is himself humbled if necessity compels
him to humble another;
Who does
not
flatter wealth,
cringe before power,
or
boast of his own
possessions or
achievements;
who speaks with frankness
but always with sincerity and
sympathy;
whose deed follows his word;
who thinks of the rights and
feelings of others, rather than
his own; and who appears
well in any company,

A man with whom honor is sacred and virtue safe.

###

30,000 Feet

Many years ago, I drafted my own short poem called "Tenpins." I was excited at the time because it was the first poem I ever got published. I started thinking about it this week while watching a track meet.

Tenpins

Strike!
He needs a spare to win.
Position... Form... Breath...
Step... Slide... Swoosh.
Crash.
The tenpin stands alone.
Again.
Position, form; breath. Step, slide, swoosh.
No crash.
He steps away.
And looks at his hand.

###

I follow, and used to teach, a writing concept called *Show, Don't Tell*. If you want the reader to think Fred is a jerk, do not tell the reader that Fred is a jerk. Rather, paint a picture of Fred berating his administrative assistance as he throws her report at her feet. Show it. Once the writer is done, the reader gets to draw their own conclusions. The interpretation of poetry is left to the reader, like any art. In this case, to make a point, I will break protocol and share (tell) my intent. In the poem above, on his first ball, every action is separated by three periods and extra space to suggest patience, rhythm, and perfect timing, something the bowler can control. On his second ball, each of these actions are rushed together in a quicker flurry, as the bowler changes and disrupts his rhythm. And yet, he steps away and looks at his hand as if it is an unattached stranger and the one to blame for the error. The bowler does not even have a name because he lacks identity and responsibility. I have seen bowlers do this a lot and it always implied a lack of taking full responsibility to me. There was no ownership.

Recently, I was able to witness a glorious example of the opposite. This time, an athlete shows her heart and takes responsibility. On Aug 26, 2023, during the World Athletics Championship, Dutch athlete Femke Bol was in the lead when she stumbled and fell during the 4x400m mixed relay final ten feet from the finish line.[71] As a result, the American sprinter passed her, and the United States team earned the Gold Medal. The Dutch did not receive any medal. Bol did not look at her hand or make excuses. She got up, dusted herself off and continued with the competition.

The very next day, Bol competed in the women's 4x400 meter relay. When she took the baton on the last leg, she was in a distant third place. She remained that way for most of the race. With less than one hundred meters left, her team was prepared for a Bronze Medal. But Bol dug deeper and in the final meters passed both of her competitors in dramatic fashion, winning the race and earning the Dutch the World Championship Gold Medal in the event.[72] Femke Bol showed her determination, resilience, and responsibility. She owned it.

The same concepts apply to crisis communications. We should show, not tell, and take responsibility, ownership for our actions. We can *tell* with a soundbite. We *show* by getting our hands dirty, on the ground, alongside other responders and survivors, working the response and recovery.

---

[71] *"4x440 World Athletic Championship,"* YouTube
[72] *"Must See Comeback,"* YouTube

We hear officials often tell reporters that their "thoughts and prayers" are with those impacted. That makes sense if it is sincere; but it is ignored when it is not shown

In October 2002, the D.C. sniper attacks were a series of coordinated shootings that occurred throughout the Washington metropolitan area.[73] I lived there at the time, and it was terrifying. But when Chief Charles Moose came on television, with tears in his eyes and emotion that showed his earnest heart, we were all comforted.[74]   He took responsibility, ownership, and captured the murderers.

At the macro-level, in everything we do, and our organizations promote, demonstrating true character, as well as showing that we take responsibility and ownership, are the roots that must grow strong so other characteristics may flourish.

Three Feet

If I could only teach one specific lesson to individuals on how to avoid making bad decisions, I would encourage them to watch a 28-minute video, published in 1984, called the

---

[73] *"DC Sniper Attacks,"* Wikipedia
[74] *"Charles Moose,"* Wikipedia

"Abilene Paradox."[75] The video is based on both a book and article written by Jerry Harvey, a professor of management science. He describes a scenario where:

> *"...four reasonably sensible people who, of our own volition, had just taken a 106-mile trip across a godforsaken desert in a furnace-like temperature through a cloud-like dust storm to eat unpalatable food at a hole-in-the-wall cafeteria in Abilene, when none of us had really wanted to go. In fact, to be more accurate, we'd done just the opposite of what we wanted to do. The whole situation simply didn't make sense."[76]*

Whether it is good manners, groupthink, fear of speaking up, or just going with the flow, groups often decide on a course of action that nobody wants. The beauty of knowing, sharing, and teaching the *Abilene Paradox*, is so the next time you see this slippery slope evolving, you can simply ask, "Are we heading toward an *Abilene Paradox?*" Watch for this during the next few meetings you attend, and you will witness it. I have even shared this video with family and friends because it is equally effective in personal

[75] *"The Abilene Paradox,"* SMUJonesFilm
[76] *"The Abilene Paradox,"* The Management of Agreement

group dynamics. We no longer go to a bad restaurant or movie that nobody wanted.

Today and tomorrow, you do not need to read books or watch videos to understand successful human characteristics at work. Just look at your lessons from previous work positions and apply them now. If you have little work experience, ask mentors and friends to share their stories. I have learned something from every job I have ever had. We all do.

Landscaping. A common job I had as a teenager included all forms of yard work. One time I was paired with a 22-year-old man laying 50-pound grass sods on three acres of property. He gave me a tough time for making him look bad in front of the boss because I was laying down two grass sods to every one of his and I did not take breaks. I learned then to never minimize my capabilities to benefit other people's performance.

Ice Cream Shop. This place was like a local version of a Dairy Queen, but in New Hampshire, and in addition to burgers and fries in the back, of course we made lobster rolls too. I learned from my boss, Barb, how working hard and having fun are not mutually exclusive. They never were and they are not now. It was the best restaurant in town, and we laughed a lot. I also learned that the smell of raspberry ice cream makes me want to vomit.

Supermarket. At just eighteen years old I was hired as the night manager. After closing, the focus changed to stocking all the shelves. One member of my crew, Brad, was older than me because you had to be over twenty-one years-old to stock the beer. One night, I turned the corner and Brad was sitting on the floor in the aisle with a half-empty bottle of Molson Golden Ale sitting on the ground next to him. He looked up with just a bit of hesitation and claimed, "I just found it here like that." His eyes gave him away, but I knew that I could not prove otherwise. I told him that of course I believed him, but that I did not believe in coincidences and that if I ever saw him and an open bottle of beer again in the same place and time, I would report it to the Manager. I learned about second chances, patience, and that Brad was a bad liar.

Bartender. If you have never been a bartender and you wondered why some are so effective while others don't know how to make a Gimlet or an Old Fashioned, and worse still, why some can't seem to make it back around to replace your empty pint glass with another Sam Adams Lager, it usually has very little to do with what you are presently seeing. The difference is in their practice and preparedness. I made hundreds of drinks before I ever stepped behind a bar and served one. Each night I would make sure that all of the glasses were clean, the mixes fully stocked, and the garnishes cut and ready. I learned to be prepared. Well, that and that the best Old Fashioned starts with a sugar cube at the bottom of the glass and not simple syrup.

Restaurant Manager. I was an assistant manager at a family friendly restaurant for a while. As many in the business can tell you, Mother's Day is one of the worst days of the year. I had seen busy Sundays and other holidays before, but that day is like none other. I rolled up my sleeves and washed pots and pans. I made chocolate banana shakes. I refilled the water glasses. I swept the floors. I learned the value of teamwork and leading by example. The skillet meals were surprisingly good too.

Teacher. I taught high school English for two years in two different schools. In the first one, we built an 18th century whaleboat using 18th century tools. We competed with distinction in a Shakespeare festival against the prestigious Exeter Academy. I was an assistant coach of the Track Team. I taught Theater and Debate, and even helped a small bit with the school play, "You're a Good Man, Charlie Brown." The next year I transitioned to a bigger school with a slightly larger, but economically essential, rise in pay. The students were every bit as amazing. But it was the kind of school where lesson plans were regimented, and you had to be on the right chapter of the textbook by the right day. This time, I learned that we must dare to do remarkable things. I also learned that Shakespeare's Sonnet 18 is just as lovely when spoken in Japanese.

Vice President, Public Relations Firm. I took the job, in part, because I thought the position title sounded so cool. They deserved better. Less than two months in I went to attend a meeting and the conference room was empty. After almost ten minutes beyond the starting time, I left and assumed I had the wrong time or place. Later in the day I ran into a colleague who asked where I was. When I told him, he confirmed that I was in the right place and time. He chuckled that the rest of the group must have just missed me as they began trickling in ten minutes after the hour. I had learned in a previous position in the Army that if you are not five minutes early, you are five minutes late. Punctuality matters. It is the way you show respect for others and their time.

Beltway Bandit Contractor/Consultant. I only lasted at this job for two months, as I had also applied to FEMA and soon got the offer. But my experience here was different than at the PR firm. My friend John was already working there and quickly showed me the ropes. It was extremely easy to catch on because the second you signed on to your computer you were welcomed to a simple dashboard that gave you access to everything at just one click. Training. Templates. News. Internet. Social Media. HR. More. One-stop shop and incredibly intuitive. I did not know the phrase then, but I have cited it countless times since as a positive example of Knowledge Management, which is loosely defined as having technology serve the mission and not the mission serve technology. It is a rare and beautiful thing.

Job experiences are not the only place to find characteristics to emulate. With empathy, examples show up in all kinds of places.

Empathy deserves a story too. It is also something you can exercise today. You might think this is a story about humor, but that is secondary. Pay attention to the empathy, or lack thereof.

Singer and actor, Bing Crosby died of a heart attack on October 14, 1977, right after completing a round of golf. Soon after, a joke spread that, "he lost to his partner by one stroke." On January 28, 1986, the American Space Shuttle Challenger Seven exploded. Shortly, the joke came out, "What does NASA stand for? Need Another Seven Astronauts."

They had friends and families. Everyone forgot about their lives. And we have continued to lose more empathy over the years. Because we fail to focus on humanity.

The lives. There were five lives lost on the Titanic Submersible that imploded in June 2023.[77] That gets lost sometimes in the coverage and the public response. There have been many articles written about the technology, the unreliable safeguards, the efforts to try to save and later recover, and the entitlement of rich people to undergo such a journey. This last one irks me.

And I do not put the blame for this one on mainstream media. While we learned over time that these souls had already perished, jokes and memes were plastering the internet even when we thought they may still be alive. They continued swiftly after their deaths were confirmed. One meme declared, "Billionaires are good people…down deep." Another one joked, "Props to the Titanic…for still drowning rich people after 111 years." I will not go on. You can search for them if that is your thing.

In the case of the submersible, humor was flying around when they still might have been alive.

---

[77] *"Timeline of the Titanic Sub,"* CNN

While that factor is not comparable to the earlier examples (we did not know Crosby and the astronauts were about to die), do we have many examples of jokes about people about to die? Thankfully, I cannot think of any. The lack of empathy is so much worse than the examples of Cosby and NASA. The submersible jokes were a direct attack on the people and their attributes, in this case wealth. Bing's joke was a play on words about golf. Not about him. The NASA joke was a play on the acronym. Not a reference to any of the individuals. But have we as a society dropped to such a level of depravity that jokes have surpassed basic human compassion and empathy? And is it funny when rich people die tragically? Even the 19-year-old? Do we have to bring others down to lift ourselves up?

By the way, the lost souls from this tragedy, who all had family and friends, the five people who never did anything personally to hurt the millions who have laughed at their tragic demise, are: Hamish Harding, Stockton Rush, Suleman Dawood with his father, Shahzada Dawood, and Paul-Henri Nargeolet.[78] May they rest in peace. Empathy is a critical human characteristic for communicators.

---

[78] *"Tribute paid to Titan Five,"* CNN

In closing, to reassess your human characteristics, what you stand for, what you value, also consider writing your own leadership philosophy, even if nobody works for you yet. Ask other leaders for a copy of theirs. The essential human characteristics will stand out. Here are a few bullets from mine, not previously addressed.

- Survivors are our first priority.
- Do not hate the media; do not love them.
- Do not say in 20 minutes what you can say in 20 seconds.
- Always be an active participant.
- Be responsive.
- Be passionate.
- Do not hold grudges.
- Bad news does not get better with age.
- Underwrite honest mistakes and informed risk-taking.
- Deadlines are a point of failure, not an objective.
- Information needs to be accessible in order to be actionable.
- Manage resources with tenacious stewardship, protecting the institution and investment.

That is quite a handful of characteristics and there are more to follow. Pat yourself on the back

for the ones you do well. Explore the ones you do
not.

###

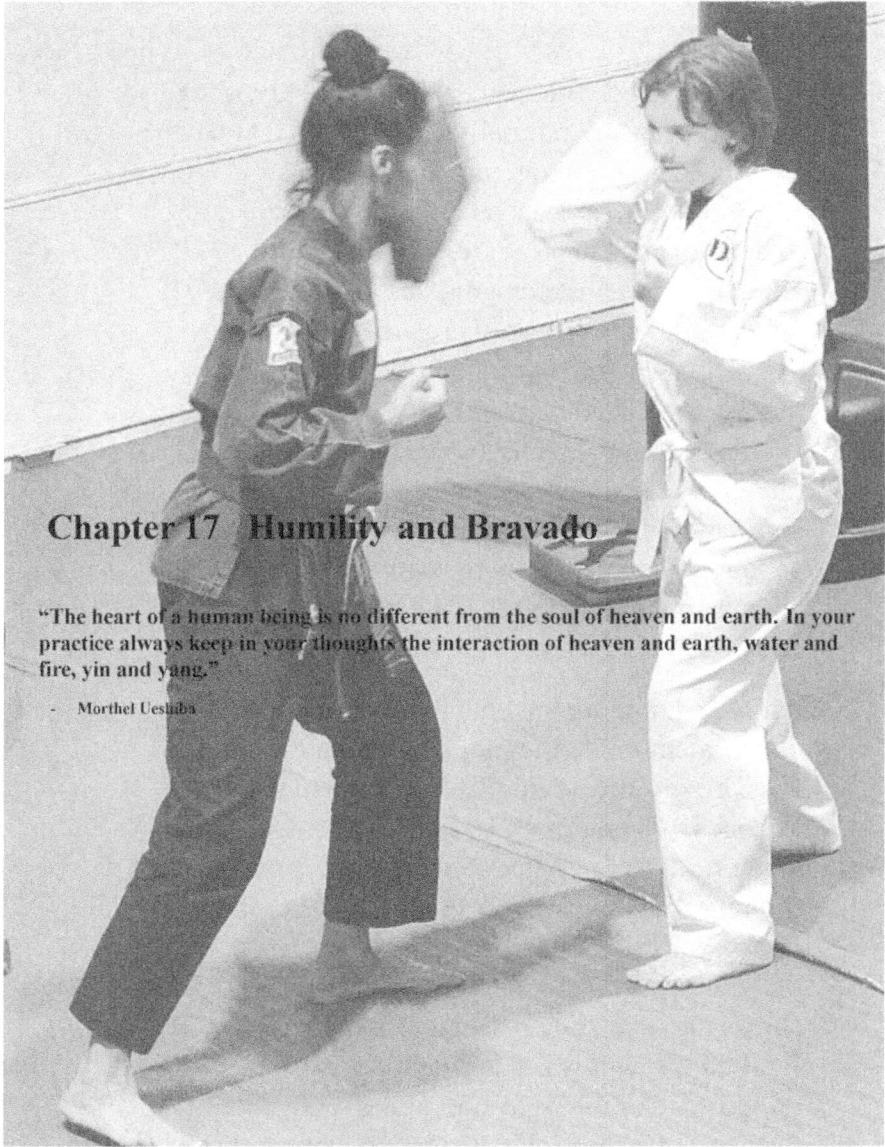

Chapter 17   Humility and Bravado

"The heart of a human being is no different from the soul of heaven and earth. In your practice always keep in your thoughts the interaction of heaven and earth, water and fire, yin and yang."

- Morthel Ueshiba

Chapter 17   Humility and Bravado by Dan Stoneking

I am fascinated with bears. The bear is my spirit animal. Bears are normally shy animals that have truly little desire to interact with humans. However, if their space is invaded, they are quick to defend and can be aggressive. Our spirit animals, or totems, can guide us and protect us. If you do not know yours, there are many quizzes online that can help you find out. I have met many people who believe that their spirit animal is a dog or a cat. But it goes deeper and different than that bond. Without a quiz, each person's spirit animal is one that they feel drawn to but cannot explain why. There is an innate connection. I have felt that with bears since an early age.

And in adulthood, the bond has become tighter due to memorable life moments. Many years ago, I visited my sister Jenny at her home in the Poconos. One morning I went for a long run along rural roads. After about ten miles I was running back towards her home. I was running on the left side of the road, against traffic (if there was any). I saw something move slightly across the road and up ahead of me. Once I had focused, I saw it was a grown black bear sitting on the edge of the right side of the road, about twenty yards ahead. I was running slow at this point, but my mind was racing. Should I turn around and go back the way I came? Should I become still? And my inner voice was screaming at me to not stare at the bear. But I did stare. And I kept slowly running forward. When I came abreast of him, only separated by the narrow country road, our eyes remained locked on each other. As I finally passed, I continued my run back to Jenny's house, never looking back. I was at complete peace and knew I was safe.

On another occasion, I was living alone and flipping channels on the TV. I came across a documentary that was just starting on PBS that promised no commercial interruptions. It was a random moment with a remote. I am typically not a fan of documentaries (I know, shame on me). And since the remote in those days could not pause a movie, I was fairly sure I would want a snack or to go to the bathroom before the movie was over. But then the title came on the screen, "Grizzly Man," directed by Werner Herzog.[79] This special version included bonus footage and interviews, resulting in more than three full hours uninterrupted. I set the remote on the table and watched. Other than my mouth half open, I do not think I flinched for the entire show. Credits

---

[79] *"Grizzly Man,"* IMDb

were rolling up, and I still could not move. I was spellbound.

Lastly, I had the opportunity as a soldier to get a ride on a Black Hawk helicopter in Alaska as we were learning about drug interdiction missions. At one point the pilot exclaimed over the headphones, "Wow, take a look at that!" As he spoke, he rotated the helicopter on the left side, my side, facing the stream not far below. I was belted in and secure, but there were no doors. I looked right below me, and God as my witness, I saw a massive Brown Bear in the stream, catch a salmon in his mouth, look up, and stare at me (or the helicopter) in defiance. Again, my eyes locked eyes with a bear. To this day, it was the most amazing visual I have ever encountered.

I have shared those experiences many times verbally, but I have never written them down. While thrilling and deeply memorable, they are but a backdrop to the greatest lesson I learned from bears. They have an unrivaled balance, a yin and a yang, between shy and aggressive, or mild and bold, or what I have coined over the years, a natural balance between humility and bravado. I have learned to bring a similar balance into risk and crisis communications. Be a bear.

30,000 Feet

In my experience, most communicators tend to be one or the other. It is also natural that we have a comfort zone for our behavior. And in life, I do not think there is anything particularly wrong with being primarily humble or bold. But each has a price to pay.

From 2004 until 2012, Fox aired a drama show called "House."[80] The main character, Dr. Gregory House, was bold, brash, and full of bravado. Everyone respected him, but few people liked him. His one friend was the character Dr. James Wilson. Everyone liked Dr. Wilson, but they did not truly respect him in the way they did Dr. House. They were the yin to the other's yang.

In crisis communications, either of those singular traits in a communicator is a problem. Communicators that are meek, mild, and shy can get bulldozed by a reporter. Conversely, coming across too bold or appearing arrogant can offend and put people off. Balance is the key, and it is often dictated by the question. For example:

Reporter: Are you all in charge of this response and recovery?

Bear: Actually, we are just one part of a big team, local, state, federal, voluntary

---

[80] *"House,"* IMDb

organizations, working together to help survivors. [**Humility**]

Reporter: Where have you all been? We are hearing that you have not accomplished anything in the last few days. Is this just another example of bureaucracy?

Bear: Actually, we were on the ground with our partners before the storm, we are here today, and we will be here tomorrow and every day until the community recovers. We have 150 people deployed, provided $1.5 million in support, and we have assisted 341 survivors so far at our recovery center. Your news station can be part of the solution by sharing our information and keeping survivors informed. [**Bravado**]

It is a subtle, seasoned, and nuanced balance. It is essential to be self-aware and to know the tendencies of each member of the team. Some will need to soften; others will need to build their courage and confidence. Both tools are necessary in the crisis communications toolbox. It takes time to change. Proceed with caution. Spoiler alert – things did not turn out very well for the guy in "Grizzly Man."

Three Feet

In each new position, I begin by asking each member or my team which way they think they lean, then I offer my honest assessment, and we work to bring them towards the middle, capable of executing both styles. For what it is worth, I have seen this balance work well as a customer, an athlete, and even in personal relationships. You will not see a chapter like this in any other crisis communications book, and yet, this might be the most important chapter you read, elevating communications with all stakeholders, internal, external, and personal.

How to be Humble:

- Admit mistakes. Some folks think this is a sign of weakness and I guess that would be true if you were making mistakes all day long. The admissions would become tedious and put a spotlight on your weak performance. But you know that is not the case. The other day I had to discipline my teenage daughter for a recent series of thoughtless and rude behavior. When I was done, she asked if she could respond. I thought for sure that she would try to form some kind of defense that would irritate me further. Instead, she accepted responsibility, apologized, and vowed to do better. And she did. Her response stopped me in my tracks and made me respect her more. Nice job, Ivy.

- <u>Lose sometimes</u>. I had a boss at one point in my career who counseled me, "Dan, when you are a boss, you have the power, but you don't have to wield that power every single time." I still remember that more than 20 years later. And it has served me well. Letting others win on occasion, as long as it is not harmful to the organization's mission or reputation, is empowering.
- <u>Collaborate</u>. Leading and controlling others all of the time is off-putting. Collaboration is not a strong suit for everyone, but when you can do it and approach it with a sense of building others up, that kindness will be seen as a strength.
- <u>Learn</u>. Professional reading, taking classes, attending seminars, asking a colleague to teach you something, all demonstrate your selfless commitment to personal and professional growth. I once had a photographer who worked for me that did not appreciate my input and feedback on the content of his photos. One day, I asked him if he could spend a few hours with me and teach me about lighting, which was one of my weaknesses. I learned a lot that day, but I also earned back his trust and respect.

- <u>Listen</u>. Easy, right? You do it every day, right? Do you ever find yourself starting to speak before the other person has finished? Are you formulating your response in your head while they are speaking? Today or tomorrow, try to just have two conversations where your only goal is to listen, hear, and consume. If you have to say anything, make it simple questions to achieve clarity of understanding (not to find a gap in their idea). At the end, sum up what you think you heard, repeat it back and ask if you understood correctly. Just for two conversations. Go ahead now if you like. I will wait. If you found that challenging, then you have found an opportunity for focus and improvement.
- <u>Give credit</u>. I do not know if it was simply good luck, or how my parents raised me, but even though overall my inclinations are on the bravado side, I naturally and inherently always give credit to whoever inspired and/or completed the work. One of my more common emails to my boss would start off saying "I am sharing this read ahead package that Melissa put together, which I think is amazing...," or "Here is Amanda's latest Newsletter and it is her

best one yet ...." By giving credit you don't lose anything, but you gain the respect from the people who earned it. I am shocked every time I am in a leadership meeting and one of the other Directors submits something without identifying who on their team actually performed the work. Do not be that person.

- Be curious. Find out more about your boss, your peers, your team. Ask what inspired a promising idea. Encourage them to share what motivates them. Ask reporters about their background and what kind of stories they like to write. People love to talk about themselves, so giving them the opportunity will make them love you more.

- Self-deprecating. I was being interviewed for a job one time and we got to that classic question where they asked me "What's your biggest weakness?" I responded quickly and honestly that I fully expected that I would get lost after the interview trying to leave the building. They laughed. We moved on to another question. I was hired. A few weeks later I was staffing the principal on a trip to a news agency. We had a driver. The principal asked me where we were going

and how long it would take to get there. I
reminded him that when he interviewed
me, I admitted that I cannot even find my
way out of a building, let alone across
Washington, DC. He laughed and never
asked me for directions again. I often
share my two other big weaknesses,
anything medical and anything financial.
They are foreign languages to me. Being
self-deprecating about these issues solves
three problems. First, I have managed
expectations on my weaknesses. Second,
when I tell people that I am a faster
writer, more creative public speaker, and
more responsive than most, I am trusted
without appearing arrogant. Third, and
finally, I am respected for being a person
of my word without fear of letting others
down.

- Do not have a shit list. When I was
  Company Commander in the Army, I met
  another commander who actually had a
  written shit list. This was a list of soldiers
  who had failed in some way, caused
  problems, and whom the commander
  planned to dispatch as soon as possible. I
  thought it was the dumbest thing I ever
  heard. That same year, I happened to have
  a soldier that I had to punish for one thing
  and a few months later gave an award for

a different thing. My boss challenged me
for not being consistent. I defended my
action by demonstrating that one thing
had nothing to do with another.
Throughout the rest of my career, I have
seen far too many leaders, even if they
did not actually write them down, who
have shit lists. That says more about the
leaders' failures than it does about the
employees. True and humble leaders
catch people doing something right, even
if they have done wrong before.

If everything on this humble list sounds easy and
second nature to you, then the next list here is
where you need to focus your efforts. If you find
yourself thinking you are an A+ in humility, you
are too humble. Conversely, if you found
yourself uncomfortable about some of those
ideas, please try them and enjoy the following list
that may be your comfort zone, and one you
might need to tone down.

How to demonstrate Bravado:

- Speak up. If you habitually attend
  meetings and seldom speak up, you have
  a problem. If you hear an idea and you
  find flaws in the logic or gaps of
  information and you do not speak up, you
  have a problem. If you are one of seven to

nine people in an hour-long meeting and you never say a thing, you are too humble. The trick is to find the right time to speak, in a genuine way, where you can provide value. Life immediately gives you a report card. If others look confused and there is an awkward silence before they shift to more conversation without addressing your comment, then you need to work more on this skill. Seek out a mentor or a peer. On the other hand, if you get immediate feedback or praise, then you have established yourself. I love it at meetings when after I speak, others will either agree or comment "Like Dan said...." Caution - if you are the person who speaks up seven times in that meeting (unless you are supposed to be leading the topic) then you have over-extended and need to throttle back.

- Courage. I love the quote by actor Ruth Gordon, "Courage is like a muscle. We strengthen it with use." If you lack demonstrable courage, start small, both at work and at home. I recently performed at a spoken word event in Delaware. My first time. I was so scared. I persevered and made it through. The people were so nice and receptive. It reminded me that fear is what happens before something.

Courage takes you through it. But nobody ever talks about what comes after. You survive. You often reap praise and recognition. And you become stronger. I took it up a notch and put a video of me singing a song, which I wrote myself, on Facebook. I know that I am not a good singer at all, but I thought since I wrote the song, people would not know if I was off key. I got a few compliments and a few likes. But I also received some criticism. It stung. But as I look back, it was well worth it. I have a saying I have used often since I was a high school English teacher and through my emergency management career, "Do the hard right over the easy wrong." That is how you build integrity at work. Take the chance, be bold and courageous. Then watch what happens immediately after and how you feel a week after. That will motivate you to strengthen that muscle even more."

- Make alliances. When I knew an important and divisive issue was going to come up in a meeting, I would seek out like minded colleagues *before* the meeting to ensure we would back each other up. There is power and bravado in numbers. And if you are the one forming the alliance, you have demonstrated even more bravado. Just use them for good.

- <u>Be a mentor</u>. I am all about being a mentee as well, but it is when you become a mentor that your boldness can shine. You are helping and leading someone else. And you do not have to be in a leadership position to do it. Whatever you do, you have skills that someone else does not have. It can be formal or informal, professional or personal. If you commit to it and do your best, your mentee will respect you, word will get around, and more will want your counsel. This might be the easiest of all the steps to build your bravado.

- <u>Affirmations</u>. I used to be a bit jaded about affirmations. In my younger years they seemed silly and superfluous. I was wrong. They exist because they work. Find the messages you need and print out memes or posters and put them around where you work. Once a day for a few weeks arrive at your desk and before you turn on your computer simply say "I am bold. I am strong. I can manage anything that comes my way today." That takes about six seconds. I dare you. Do not doubt whether it will work; ask yourself what you have to lose? Nobody else has to know. I will not tell anyone. And if that does not work, do an internet video search for Stuart Smalley telling himself, "I'm Good Enough, I'm Smart Enough, and Doggone It, People Like Me!" At least you will get a laugh.

- <u>Embrace failure</u>. This one is the hardest to do but also reaps the greatest benefits. I do not mean try to fail. I mean, try to do everything that you think should be done, take every clever idea and try to make it happen. You may try eight things and only two succeed, but those two will earn you recognition and achievement. Your failures prove you have the strength to try and persevere. You just need a few guidelines. Do not fail on things assigned by the boss. And when you try those ten things that you think will be cool and valuable to achieve, do not tell anyone, especially the boss, that you are trying to do them. All the boss will see are the two successes once you promote them. The failures will teach you and give you strength.
- <u>Dare to be great</u>. In the end, it all becomes a matter of will, desire, and direction. You know what greatness looks like in your job and at your organization. If it is not clear, it is that thing that you

will want to brag about to family and friends. Write it down. Read it. Read it repeatedly. Do it. Be that person. Nobody ever wants to grow old and tell their grandchildren about mediocrity.

Remember, you never need to wonder if you suffer from too much humility or too much bravado. Just ask. Someone will tell you. And then find that balance. Be the bear.

###

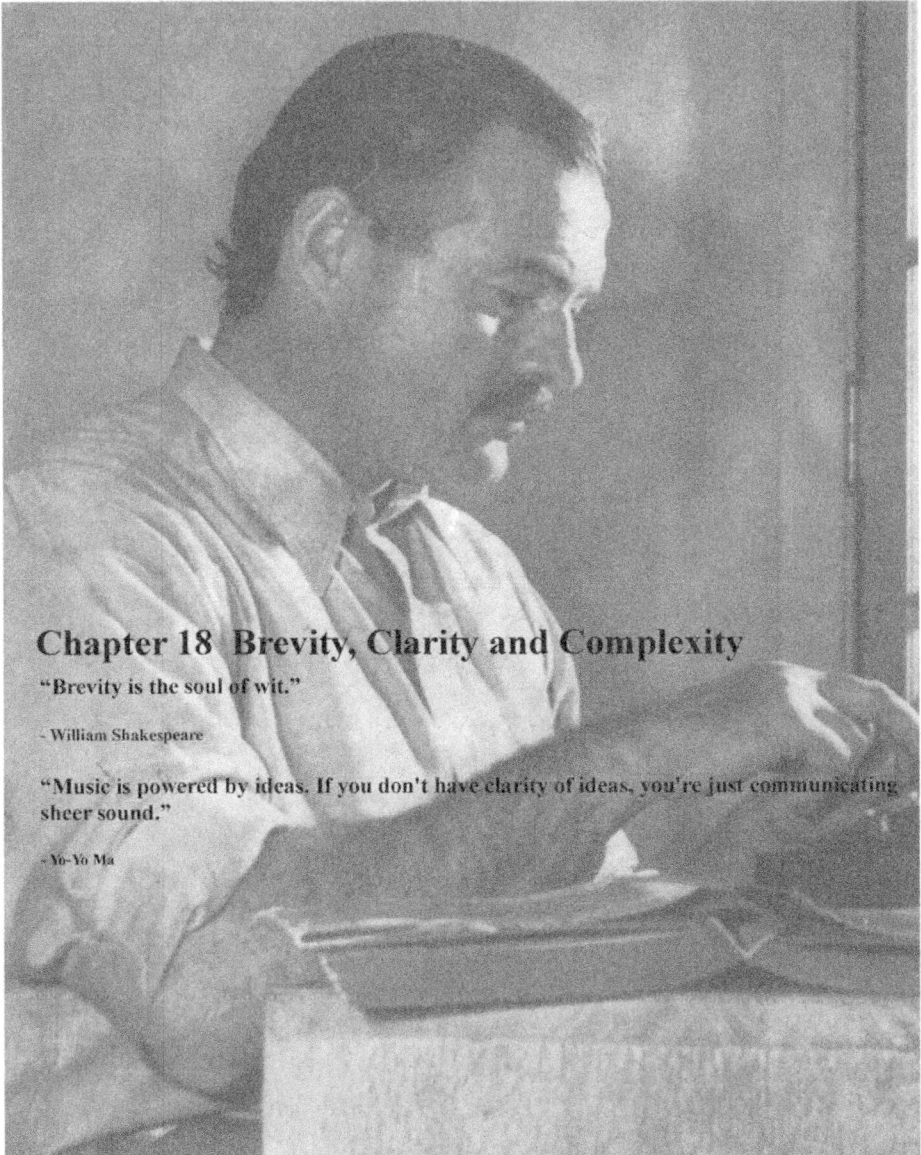

Chapter 18 Brevity, Clarity and Complexity

"Brevity is the soul of wit."

- William Shakespeare

"Music is powered by ideas. If you don't have clarity of ideas, you're just communicating sheer sound."

- Yo-Yo Ma

Chapter 18   Brevity, Clarity, and Complexity
by Dan Stoneking

The Lord's Prayer has **56 words**. Lincoln's Gettysburg Address has **266 words**. The Ten Commandments has **297 words**. The Declaration of Independence has **300 words**. The 2022 USDA Guide for Shell Egg Grading Procedures (voluntary program) has **24,036 words**.[81]

Yep. Let that sink in.

30,000 Feet

There is this great fable, told by different people in diverse ways about a man who had a chalk sign in front of his shop that said' "Fresh Fish Sold Here." One customer suggested that one could assume the fish were fresh. The sign became, "Fish Sold Here." Later, another remarked that of course the fish were being sold and not given away. "Fish Here." Yet another asked, where else would the fish be? "Fish." Finally, a customer looked at the sign and proclaimed. "'Fish?' No kidding. I am standing right here. I can smell them, can't I?" Finally, the sign was wiped clean. Later, the shop owner's wife noticed they had no customers and chastised her husband for erasing the sign.

---

[81] *"700 Series: Shell Egg Grader Procedures,"* USDA

The moral and the key is to strike a balance. I just told that story in less words than anywhere else I could find it. You still understood it.

Three Feet

Brevity is about respecting everyone's time. Brevity avoids redundancy. Brevity can take ten seconds (attention span). Brevity in email does not need the scroll bar.

Clarity ensures the receiver understands the sender. Clarity does not assume. Clarity identifies the action and the actor. Clarity loves Who, What, When, Why, and Where.

Complexity is confusing and hard to understand. A crisis response can be complex. Those impacted want simple answers. The crisis communicator needs to translate complexity into simplicity.

This is the shortest chapter in this book, clear, and not complex (**298 words**).

###

Chapter 19 Adhocratic Risk

"The disease which inflicts bureaucracy and what they usually die from is routine."

- John Stuart Mill

"Bureaucracy defends the status quo long past the time when the quo has lost its status."

- Laurence J. Peter

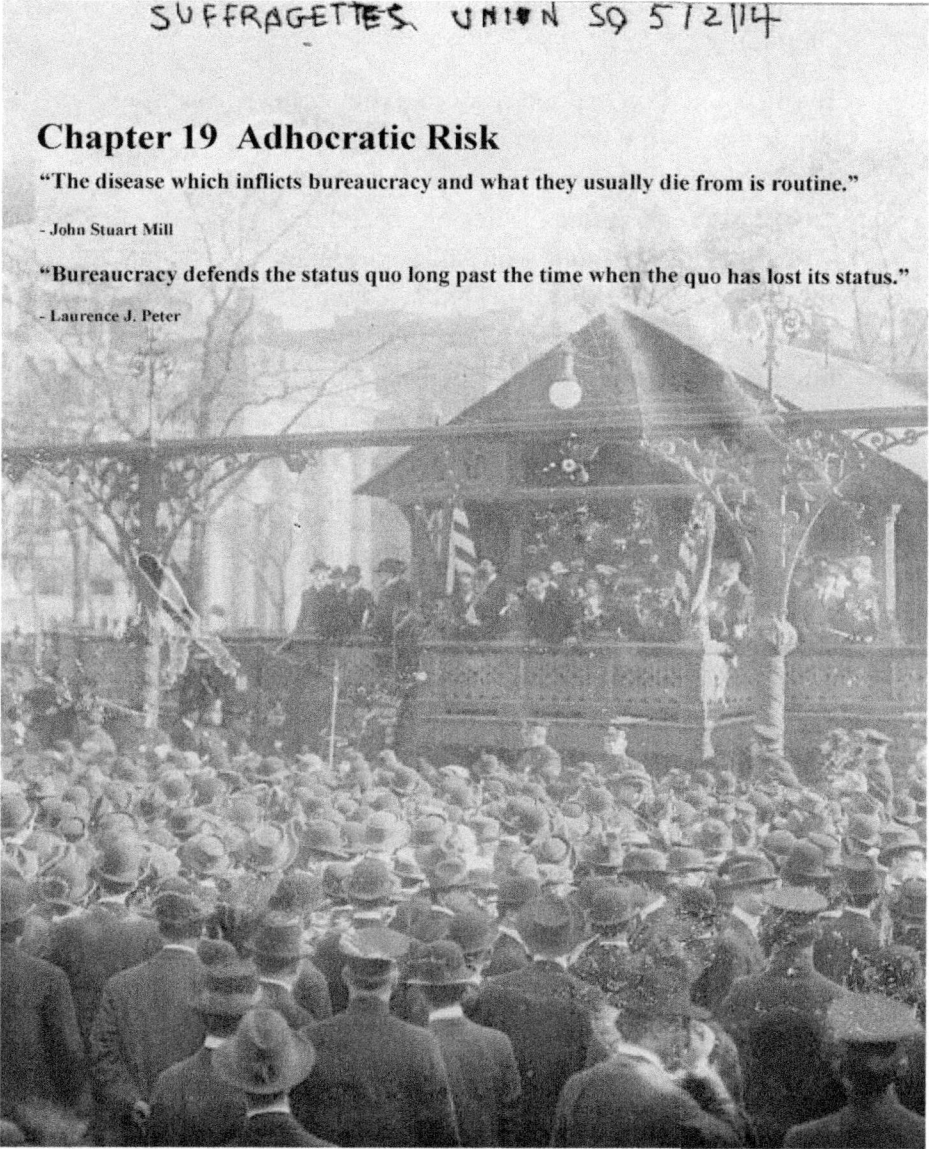

Chapter 19   Adhocratic Risk by Dan Stoneking

If you looked up "adhocracy" in a dictionary, you would find some version of "a flexible, adaptable, and informal organizational structure without bureaucratic policies or procedures." If you looked up Adhocrat or Adhocratic, you might not even find them. That is a shame, because we certainly have bureaucracy, bureaucrats, and bureaucratic offices. They desperately need a counterpoint. Even the definition of adhocracy sounds a bit bureaucratic.

I would define adhocracy as "having the *personal* courage to take the risks to achieve great results in spite of all the crap in your way." That is what led me to my philosophy of *Adhocratic Risk*. I did an internet search soon after I coined the term to see if anyone had beaten me to it. Nothing came up. The amalgamation of the two terms reminds us that you cannot have one without the other, even using the boring original definition above. I italicized *personal* in my definition to emphasize that I am not addressing organizational culture. I am challenging you to oppose organizational culture where necessary to achieve the mission in spite of the organization.

Apple, Google, Spotify and Tesla are often described as having a culture of adhocracy, because of the distinct types of autonomy, flexibility, and equality they afford in their models.[82] If you work for one of those companies, you may not need to risk much at all. But for much of the rest of the corporate world and all of the public sector, it all begins with risk.

30,000 Feet

There are countless risk assessment models and matrices that you could search and review. They address two simple factors, probability and risk. For our purposes, as crisis communicators pushing the envelope with our adhocratic risk, let us define *probability* as the chances that you will get caught going against the bureaucratic grain. And, for us, the *impact* would be the price we have to pay for our behavior, anywhere from a scolding, up to official admonishment at the highest level of impact.

Each of us would have different scenarios, so you would have to fill those in for yourself. But I have developed this simple adhocratic risk assessment decision matrix for you. All you need to do is swap out the scenario.

---

[82] *"Adhocracy Cultures."* Academy to Innovate HR

So, you are thinking of moving into a dog-friendly neighborhood, and you are wondering what risks may be ahead of you….

The Scenario	The Risk	The Decision
A Chihuahua that lives three blocks away, nipping at your shoelaces	Low Probability Low Impact	Take the risk
A Chihuahua in your house, nipping at your shoelaces	High Probability Low Impact	Take the risk
A Pit Bull bred for fighting secured behind your neighbor's iron fence and on a choke chain leash, hurting you	Low Probability High Impact	Take the risk, but stay focused and continue to reevaluate
That same Pit Bull suddenly in your backyard, with saliva dripping from its mouth, as it is charging toward you.	High Probability High impact	Um, skip this one. Do not take the risk.

Three Feet

When my brother Mike graduated college, with a degree in architecture, he returned home to our small town in New Hampshire and began working for a local architect. It was *fine*. But *fine* is not what he wanted with his whole life and dreams ahead of him. So, one day, after giving proper notice, he packed his bags, and with only a few dollars in his pocket, and no job offers, he hitched a ride to Philadelphia to be a roommate with some of his college friends and pursue his dreams. Forty years later, he is still an architect, loves his job, and never plans to retire.

I was so impressed and a bit envious watching the courage he possessed to do something so daring with no safety net. I had always wanted to be a high school English Teacher, but found myself ten years into an Army career, motivated initially by scholarship. I kept wondering about *what ifs* and missed opportunities. I kept thinking about Mike. So, one day, I did it. With little money, a wife, and a son, I left the Army, got my teaching degree and found my dream. Or so I thought. I taught for two years, and while I love the time with the students to this day, the structure, requirements, and school politics, all for truly little pay, convinced me to leave the profession. And I have never returned.

So, you might think these are tales of two cities, success and failure. You would be wrong. That is the thing about risk - it is rewarding regardless of the outcome because it is about ownership, empowerment, and accountability. I will forever be grateful for my experience, but even more so for having done it. The courage. No one can take that away from me. In addition, courage and risk are contagious. They are like tattoos, once you get one, you want more. Taking risks can also lead to greater rewards, achievements, and success. It is trite but true when they say, nothing ventured, nothing gained. If I were to cite the top ten or twenty accomplishments from my career, every single one of them began with an aversion to perspiring, dripping bureaucracy and a deep dive into the cool, brisk waters of risk.

In addition to the adhocratic risk assessment decision matrix, for crisis communicators, I have another litmus test to help you decide when to take the risk - whenever the outcome will be *meaningful, measurable, and visible.* It is possible to achieve one or a combination of these three with innovative storytelling. When you accomplish things through storytelling that are meaningful, measurable, and visible for the organization, any potential negative impacts are immediately mitigated.

An example of *meaningful* storytelling would be helping an individual survivor and/or responding helpfully to a public inquiry. It may be hard to measure and perhaps no one witnessed it, but like the starfish being thrown back into the ocean, it meant the world to that person, and is deeply meaningful.

When we cite the number of people and resources deployed to a crisis, it is certainly *measurable*, and that has value too in storytelling. But the data is not always visible and frankly, not that meaningful to most audiences either. It will not matter to the audiences if it was 447 people or 386 people deployed. It will not matter if it is 400,000 bottles of water or 500,000. But the measures are still an integral part of the story.

Under the right circumstances, embedding media into a crisis response can provide the most stunning and compelling *visible* stories. Unfortunately, in that example of storytelling, we pass the baton to the media to shape the meaning and the measures.

A good example of a double play are search and rescue efforts. Saving lives is undoubtedly *meaningful* and the number of saved souls is easily *measurable*. This is a remarkable story. However, due to operational security and austere or dangerous environments, as well as privacy, these are seldom visual (nor should they be).

My favorite example of a triple-play is promoting a Red Cross Blood Drive. Saving lives. Hundreds of liters of blood. Photos and videos of the blood drive and willing participants. ***Meaningful, measurable, and visible.***

Your homework is to find these storytelling opportunities, take them individually when you need to, but keep your eye on combination opportunities. Then overcome bureaucracy, take the risk, and make it happen.

Let me close out this chapter with one more story of adhocratic risk.

As a young Lieutenant in the early 1980's, I was a Platoon Leader and later Executive Officer for an Army Air Defense Battery. Our motto was, "If it flies, it dies." One year we competed in an international Hawk Missile firing competition off the island of Crete. Our platoon completed all of the steps to engage the target in stellar fashion, but when our tactical control officer pushed the button, the missile did not fire. The evaluators briefed us after that it was a technical issue and that points were not deducted for performance. They then gave us two options. Walk away at that point and we would set a new NATO record for the all-time high score. Or, if preferred, we could repeat the entire exercise after the technical issue was repaired, but if we did so, and lost points in the process, we risked the record and our reputation. The soldiers from Assault Platoon, Delta Company did not even flinch. We came to see the Hawk Missile fire and destroy the target. Set it up again. It reminded me of the Boston Red Sox great, Ted Williams, who, when faced with a similar decision, stepped up to bat at the last game of the season in 1941, a story I heard from my Grandpa often. His batting average was hovering right over .400, which, if he stopped then, would be an all-time record. But if he went to bat and struck out, his average would dip below the record-setting line.

Ted took the risk. We took the risk. Ted got a hit and made history with a .406 batting average. Our platoon had another miraculous performance. We saw the missile fly, and last I heard, we still had the record.

In closing, here is a whisper you should always allow to filter in your thoughts - is this an opportunity to seek forgiveness not permission?

###

Chapter 20 A Spoonful of Old School

"All that is gold does not glitter, not all those who wander are lost; the old that is strong does not wither, deep roots are not reached by the frost."

- J. R. R. Tolkien

Chapter 20   A Spoonful of Old School by Dan Stoneking

I ran track in high school. I was a sprinter. It was back in the day when races were measured by yards. I ran the 100, 220, and 440. Once my older brother graduated, I won more often than not, and I was the fastest one on the team. During my senior year, a new student transferred to our school. His name was Tim. All Fall and Winter, Tim bragged about how fast he was and the times he raced in his old school. When track season finally came, he looked great in practice. He had great form and bolted out of the starting blocks. We had not competed against each other yet, but I have to be honest and admit that I was a bit intimidated.

One evening at home, I mentioned to my dad that Tim was psyching me out. My dad quickly slammed that idea. There is no such thing, he told me. You get in the blocks, the gun goes off, and you run faster. That is it. 'Psyching out' has nothing to do with it. My dad was old school. And he was right.

By the next year we were building our home on the shores of Lake Winnipesaukee, in New Hampshire. Every step of the way, whether measuring, sawing or constructing, my dad always had a tattered yellow legal pad and a carpenter's pencil. That is it. No blueprints, no guide, no instructions from the materials. He was old school.

If the washer broke, he fixed it. If he wanted corn on the cob, he planted it. He served his country at war and never spoke about it. Old school.

I have thought about that often over the last many years. I love seeing the diversity of what every generation brings differently to the office. You cannot spend much time on social media without seeing memes between millennials and boomers. They are funny. I have seen versions where both parties are the butt of the joke. But in the work environment, I have seen firsthand that recent technologies are favored consistently, even when they are measurably less effective. For example, if I need to approve an old school document, it would end up in my in-box with a sticker note where I should sign. I would pick it up, sign it and move it to the out box. Seven seconds. More recently, those documents come through electronically on a software program. I have to log-in, type in my user identification and password, go to the right section, scroll until I find the right document, open the document, sign the document, sometimes an additional password is required here, save the document to my desktop, upload the signed document again, select the next person to send it to, type in their email address, send it, and exit the program. Four minutes, And that is when there are no glitches (and there often are glitches). Same with time and attendance. We used to insert our time cards to punch the clock. The current process is so laborious I do not even want to type all the steps.

To be clear, I am not advocating only choosing old school options; I am simply suggesting that we should not discard them on those occasions when they are more efficient, more effective, and can reach different audiences. And even then, I do not advocate old school procedures *instead* of newer methods; I encourage them *in addition* to the cool new methods. Keep this in mind - Generation A, Generation Z, Millennials, Generation X, and Boomers, ALL bring something to the table. But here is where Boomers are different - they are the generation that will soon all be gone from the workforce. Consider some old school strategies and tactics to include in your toolbox before none of the Boomers are left.

30,000 Feet

I have spent much of the last few decades teaching crisis communications. An important aspect to that is learning how to shape the environment. I used this example from the 1957 movie, "Bridge on the River Kwai." [83]   In the movie a Japanese warden is making the prisoners, led by a British Colonel, to build a bridge that will help the Japanese move resources. The Colonel complies in leading his men because he wants to be professional in everything he does, even in confinement. In the end, an escaped American prisoner comes back to blow up the bridge. I compare the warden to the media, and the Colonel to the audiences, and the American prisoner to the crisis communicator. The others thought they were shaping the environment, but he did.

That worked great until one day I used it and one of the students said, "that movie is so old school." As we spoke further, I learned that he was the only one in the class who had ever even heard of the movie, let alone seen it. I went too far old school as it did not relate. I started using the movie "Titanic" after that. Then "Harry Potter." More recently. The "Avatar" movies. My point, again for emphasis, is not to go old school without thought or reason but remain open-minded when it can help your organization. Here are some strategic examples your organization can adopt and adapt.

---

[83] *"The Bridge on the River Kwai,"* IMDb

Call. A colleague in Texas once told me that he wished he had a contact for Albertsons Supermarkets, because they had forty-four stores in the state and they would be a good partner for messaging to employees and customers, before and during disasters. I got off that call. Went to the website for Albertsons and clicked on Contact Us. I got on the phone with someone who redirected me to someone else. Within the hour we had a relationship with the chain of stores, and they agreed to collaborate with us on messaging. I did this kind of thing often, but this one stands out because another colleague was with me in Washington DC and asked me, before I tried and succeeded, how I could connect with Albertsons when the person in Texas could not. I told him that I was going to use a tool that my Texas counterpart had forgotten - I was going to make a few phone calls until I found the right person.

Visit. During COVID our communications team saved lives because we actually walked down streets in Philadelphia, talking to people and giving them information. We sent a vehicle with vaccines to rural Maryland. We posted flyers in apartment buildings. We invited a tribe to come all together in a time we set aside to get their vaccines. All of it made a measurable difference and contributed to saving lives. All old school.

Attend. Nobody likes flood insurance. It costs money. Our team attended town halls to answer questions and help people work through the process. I witnessed one that started off hostile, but by the end, they were thanking our insurance expert and signing up. No fancy technology involved. People talking to people.

Ask. Within our office I bought a wooden suggestion box and placed it in the break room with a pad of suggestion slips. Every two weeks we check the box, and the leader of our organization responds to every single one. We have made measurable improvements based on the suggestions we have received, to include more healthy choices in the snack machines, improved recycling, an employee engagement area, refinements to the operational tempo of meetings, more effective tools for teleworking, and more. A box.

Meet. Like many, but not all organizations, we made our meetings distraction free. No devices during the meeting. We did not have devices in the 1990's and we survived. If you have not tried this at least once, you should. The difference is palpable and remarkable. Remove technology and increase attention and active participation.

Advertise. Ten, twenty years ago, organizations used to leverage Public Service Announcements

(PSA) with zeal. Lately, they have become an afterthought. They do not seem cool enough. But they still exist, They have an audience. They are free. And it is no longer competitive to get submissions approved. Our team just did that across three states, and they were happy to help us.

Educate. When was the last time your leadership met with an Editorial Board? Ever? You can make this request with the media, and they are often receptive. It is a terrific way to help them understand the complexity of a crisis or disaster before it occurs. It builds relationships. It results in more accurate reporting. And, depending on the ground rules you establish, could also result in an immediate in depth piece on your leadership and/or organization.

Trades. An often untapped market are the trade magazines relevant to your market space. The readers are typically advocates, but they are an important audience to feed as well, since they can retell and support your stories.

None of the ideas above or below need to replace anything you are doing. They are old school opportunities that can complement and enhance your posture. There are things that each of us can change tomorrow, individually, to add a touch of old school class.

Three Feet

I met my girlfriend (*mi novia*, in Spanish) through work. We collaborated on a few important projects. She is Puerto Rican, strong, smart, and kind. I soon realized, whether in a professional or personal setting, I would approach her enthusiastically with an idea, and invariably, her first response has been to wish me a good morning, ask how my day was going, or some other form of a courtesy greeting, before she addressed the topic. Over time, I learned to adopt the same trait. Her approach was based in her culture and reminded me of how I was raised, but not who I had become.

Talk. By nature, I am an introvert. I do not often get in conversations on the elevator or in the supermarket. But in a world where we can get stuck responding to emails all day, it is becoming a lost art. Having an honest conversation with a stakeholder or colleague can unlock wonders you may not anticipate. Try to have a three to five minute conversation with someone that you normally would have been inclined to skip.

Write. We write every day. Or do we? I am not writing now; I am typing. We do not write emails or plans. We type them. So, imagine the impact this week when you hand-write a note, or better yet, mail a hand-written letter to someone. It will be impactful.

Dress. You may have heard the phrase, "dress for the job you want, not the one you have." I am not sure about that, but I do not see the downside. The more important perspective is to dress in a way that respects the people around you. In a deployment, that may be tactical gear. For a conference it may be more formal wear. I love wearing blue jeans and did it every day I could in our office. But when I went to visit a stakeholder, I always improved my dress code.

Reflect. Keep a journal. Write a blog. Meditate. There are so many ways to reflect but none of them happen without conscious choice. Reflection can help you become more self-aware, it can help you focus, and it can lead you to a better understanding of issues. It seems like nobody keeps a journal anymore. See the last chapter of this book for some of my reflections.

Manners. Remember what Mom said, "If you don't have something nice to say, don't say anything at all." Remember the "please" and "thank you." Do not interrupt others while they are speaking. I struggle with this one, but I try. When I was young my Mom would get so frustrated with me because I would wipe my mouth on my t-shirt sleeve instead of a napkin.

Horrible manners, but I still wipe my mouth off on my t-shirt sleeve. All we can do is try.

Clock. Be punctual. Being a few minutes late to meetings has become commonplace. Those who are on time have learned to be polite and considerate. Good for them. But what about the culprits who are late, especially the compulsive ones? It is rude. Whether you intend it or not, the message you are sending is that your time is more important than everyone else's.

Respond. I have a formidable reputation and I am well respected. It is not because I am smart. It is because I respond to every email and voicemail. It is not complicated but it has become a lost art. It is disrespectful to the person who reached out to you. Often, when you fail to respond another person is left hanging, without resolution to an issue. I assure you, this is the most important tip in this chapter. If you are poor at responding and you change your habit today, your reputation will significantly increase.

Relate. If you thought all of these were going to be hard, enjoy these last two. Take a longer lunch. Not a work lunch. Hang out with a friend. Read some of your books. Enjoy a nice meal. Studies have shown that taking time away actually increases productivity. I walked my new puppy twice while writing this chapter.

Relax. Take a real vacation. No computer. No work phone. It is good for your soul.

Let us be honest. You will not try all of these. Why not try a few? Just a spoonful.

###

Chapter 21   Form Follows Function

"Whether it be the sweeping eagle in his flight, or the open apple-blossom, the toiling work-horse, the blithe swan, the branching oak, the winding stream at its base, the drifting clouds, over all the coursing sun, form ever follows function, and this is the

-   Luis Sullivan, Architect 1856-1924

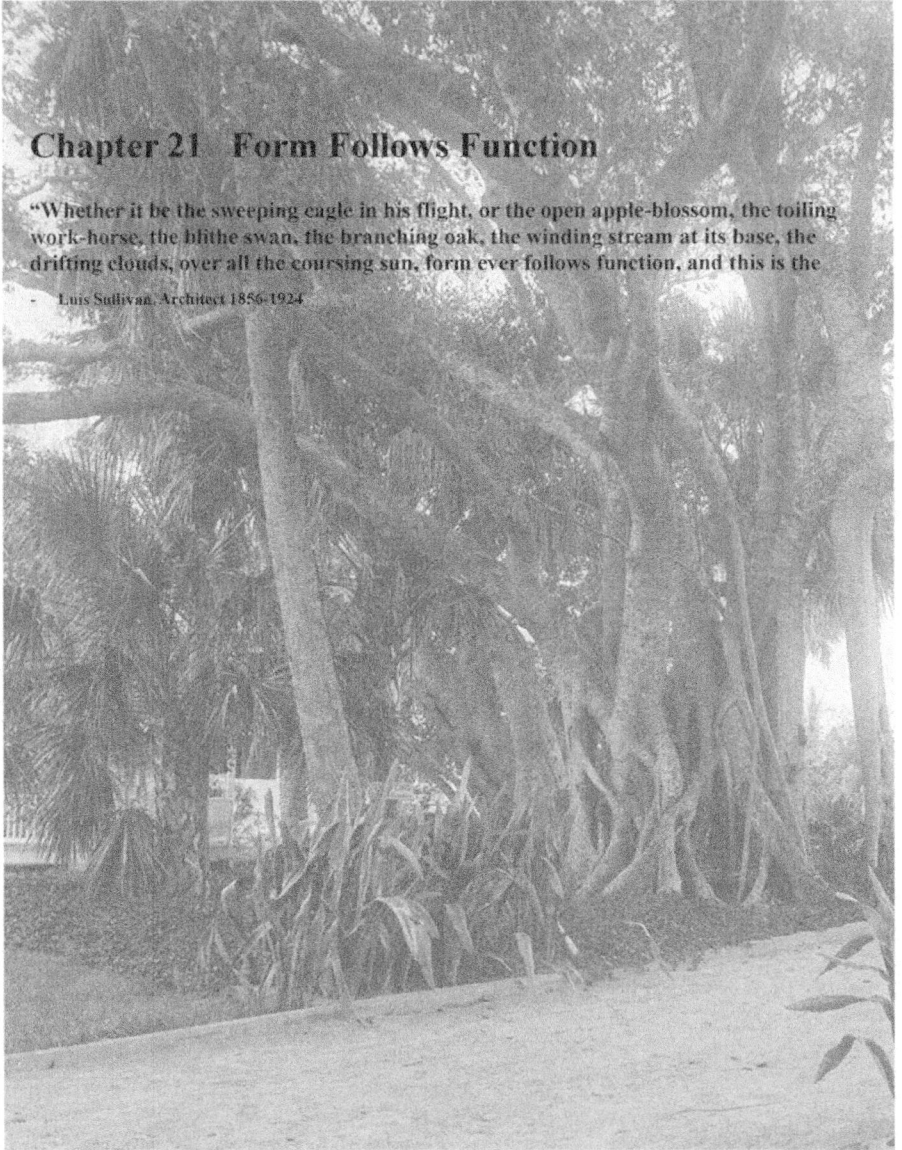

Chapter 21   Form Follows Function by Dan Stoneking

The phrase "Form Follows Function" as included in this chapter's heading, was first used by Louis Sullivan in one of his architectural articles. "This means that the functionality of the building should be a deriving factor. Major design decisions should be made based on the function, and form should be derived organically as the process goes on."[84]

We would not design an office building without bathrooms and elevators. We would not craft a blueprint for a library without considering shelving. The function has to come first. This is true of most things, including writing. I could not have crafted this book by sharing witty and random anecdotes and hope that they would somehow achieve a point. The function here is to author a book on crisis communications that helps other communicators to be successful in this profession. The forms of quotes, images, and anecdotes followed that function to paint a full picture.

In crisis communications, many of the forms are actual forms, as well as meetings, processes, bureaucracies, and emails. Often, they are also

---

[84] *"Theory In Architecture,"* Rethinking the Future

the media and mediums between the communicator and their audiences. Fortunately, there are strategic and tactical approaches that can ensure we put function first. Our function is to communicate swiftly and accurately to our communities, survivors, and constituents.

30.000 Feet

Since imagery empowers text and concepts, a few Venn Diagrams can be baked into strategic communication plans, be taught to the entire organizational team (not just strategic communicators), and even be printed and posted around the operation center as constant reminders of simplicity and focus.

Venn Diagrams are named for English logician John Venn (1834-1923) of Cambridge, who explained them in his book "Symbolic Logic" (1881).[85] While logisticians embraced them in the early 1900's, it was not until the 1960's when they began a rapid level of use up to today. Venn applied Boolean algebra to improve visual reasoning. The diagrams are used to represent relations between entities, concepts, classes, or more generally to present information.

Venn's research was complicated and evolutionary. But the result is simple. People

---

[85] *"The First Random Walk,"* Springer Link

understand them, digest them, and process them quickly, even when they do not know what they are called. They have become ubiquitous in textbooks, art, work presentations, and even humorous memes. Why? Because they work.

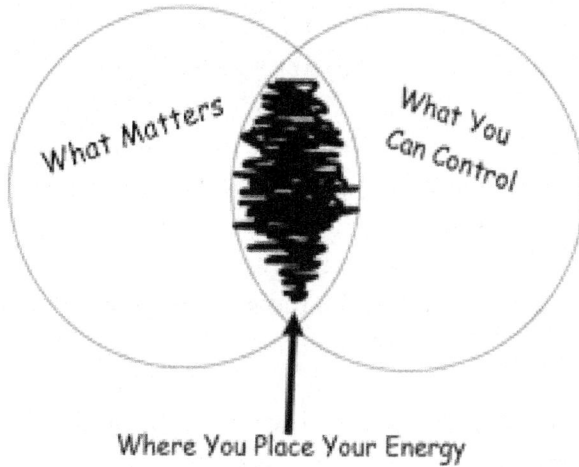

Where You Place Your Energy

I offer two similar Venn Diagrams here to advise on strategic communications. The first is more generic and can be applied to everyone in the organization. The second is more specific to communicators.

Most leaders are clear about what matters. Mission and vision statements provide that clarity and direction. Fewer leaders take the time to consider what they can actually control. Not all unwelcome news can be avoided. Not all media and audiences are malleable to being shaped or persuaded. But the intersection between what matters and what can be controlled is the sweet spot. I did not fill in examples in either diagram overlap since they differ between organizations. However, as an example, in a crisis, one thing that matters during hurricanes is that survivors have somewhere to go to avoid impact. That can also be controlled. One thing those local emergency managers can control is establishing evacuation routes. Another is to set up recovery centers. These also matter. Place your energy there. What does not matter during the crisis to those impacted is who gets credit or who provided the food at the recovery centers. And history has proven that emergency managers cannot fully control who evacuates and who does not. Nor can they control which sources of information those survivors prefer.

So, let us transition that to the crisis communicator. We want to tell the media all of the resources our agency provides, how well trained we are, how effectively we provide support, where the evacuation routes and recovery centers are located. and why it is so important that survivors adhere to local authorities. Often the media will not care about the training and effectiveness (and rightly so) near as much as the survival locations. During the life-saving stages, our self-promotion does not matter. What the media chooses to cover, we cannot control. Lifesaving and life-sustaining messages are the first priorities we want to tell, and the media will cover that. We must align our outreach priorities in the sweet spot.

Outreach Priorities

These are quick and simplistic examples. The key is to take the time to study, research, and know what falls in the overlaps in your organization.

Energy and priorities should focus within the overlaps. That is our function. Everything else is simply form. Include it in the strategy. Brief them to leadership. Rehearse them.

During a crisis, it can save time, resources and lives.

Three Feet

Let us get a little more specific and play ball at the tactical level. There are a few key games that can help us ensure that form follows function.

When my son was barely becoming a teenager, we had our share of conflict. He was learning to push boundaries while I was trying to reinforce them. He knew all of my triggers. I was getting frustrated playing one-on-one between father and son. At some point, we found basketball together. I do not remember a profound first day. It was gradual. We watched games on TV. We both liked the Celtics. He played in the local league for his age group. So, one afternoon I bought him a basketball stand. We filled the base with sand and set it up together. Not many kids his age lived nearby, so when he asked me to play, I jumped at the chance.

It was a turning point for us. We would play for hours. The first few months, I had him beat. I still had a few inches on him. But as life goes, he kept getting better and I kept getting older. By the time he was 14 years old, he was beating me on a regular basis. But he still wanted to play with me. I could not shoot to save my life, but I gave him solid defense and never went easy on him. We found mutual respect and bonded in a way that has stayed with us all our lives.

When he turned eighteen, I asked if he wanted to get tattoos together. He was afraid of the needle and pain. I would bring it up to him from time to time, but always the same response. So, I was both surprised and delighted when his 38th birthday was near, and he told me that he wanted to get basketball tattoos together. We agreed that they did not have to be the same as each other, as long as both had a basketball theme. When the day came, he got a massive arm sleeve of a slam dunk in action. I was a bit stunned that his very first tattoo was so large, but I was equally impressed. I opted for a basketball on my forearm with an EKG heartbeat running through it. Because when we started playing basketball, I could feel my heart beating for him. Our function was to find a way to bond. Ever since, we have been refining our form.

Fast forward to recently, I have been wanting to play tennis, a game I loved in my youth. In my community, just outside my kitchen window, a seldom used tennis court taunted me. I am an introvert, so finding people to play seemed daunting. I finally just put it all out there and posted a note on NextDoor social media looking for players who were as old and rusty as me. On the first day, I found three different players to join me. Once again, I was bonding through sports. I was also reminded that the function of reaching out had to precede the form of playing.

It is true what they say about sports teaching life skills like teamwork, discipline, leadership, goal setting et al. And I have learned some of all of those. But as I progressed in crisis communications, I developed my own theories inspired by these sports. In both cases, form follows function. The first is what I call The Juxtaposition of Glass and Rubber Balls. The other is The Ball in Court Theory.

The Juxtaposition of Glass and Rubber Balls

The first things you learn about balls are their purposes and their limitations. You cannot dribble a football well and a basketball will not fit into a golf hole. You learn how they function. The same is true at work. But we only have two balls to worry about, glass and rubber. This starts off simple. If you drop a glass ball, it breaks. If you drop a rubber ball, it bounces. But it gets more complicated.

You may have heard people say at work, don't juggle or drop the glass balls. But I have a different take on this concept and believe in a deeper strategic dive. In a crisis environment, glass balls can have one or more characteristics. They are often assigned from above. Of course, we are not going to drop a ball from our boss. Pure crystal. Some glass balls are highly visible. You drop one of those and the glass shards go everywhere and may even cut you. And your reputation suffers with everyone who witnessed it. When we are directly accountable for something – that is glass as well. If there is a deadline, a performance review, a budget requirement, then we simply cannot afford to juggle. But in crisis communications the most important glass ball, the Swarovski or Baccarat crystal glass ball, is anything that is survivor centric. Lifesaving and life-sustaining glass balls make the others seem like plastic.

Still, rubber balls do not get enough credit. Too often I see people only focus on the glass balls and allow some or all of the rubber ones to dribble away. That is a time management issue and a mistake. Rubber balls are often self-identified. We think of this really cool idea but keep throwing it back in the bag to focus on glass. Even if a rubber ball is not required, they can be incredibly creative and innovative. Another kind of rubber ball are those long-term projects that nobody is asking about. They are rubber until they are not.

I will posit this – that glass balls can get you in trouble, but rubber balls can make you famous. I mentioned earlier that in one of my jobs, I collaborated with a few trusted partners to create the first-in-nation National Business Emergency Operation Center. Nobody asked us to do it. In fact, we had naysayers and obstacles in the way constantly. We could have dropped it at any time, but we prevailed. Since then, I have been asked to speak about it across the nation, more models have copied it, and it has measurably contributed to saving lives.

One of your rubber balls could be a game-changer. Do not just find time, make the time.

Ball in Court Theory

Everyone I have ever worked with recognizes that I move at a fast pace. They seem shocked that my email in-box is empty when theirs has 5,000 messages, even though I receive as many, if not more. It is because I use my Ball in Court Theory. I prioritize the functions of email and task management. If you know who has the ball, where the ball is, and what to do with it, the game speeds up. Tennis works well for this analogy. There are a few clear options while I am on the court. I can serve the ball. I can volley and return the ball. I can let the ball fly out of bounds. The only thing I will not do is stand there with the ball doing nothing. And yet, we often stand with the ball at work.

As an example, I have seen communicators during a crisis take most of the day to craft a statement or a news release, even when they are capable of knocking it out in 30 minutes. And guess what happens, twenty more balls come their way while they are standing still. But just like the tennis player there are options, whether it is an ask, a task, or some other action – move the ball. You can do that by quickly completing the task if it is fast and easy. You can assign the task (now it is someone else's court). You can get a colleague to collaborate with and now you are playing doubles, which is much easier and faster. You can ask your supervisor for guidance or clarification. The ball goes back in their court for a bit while you hit other balls. And when it comes back to you, it is an easier ball to hit. You can take a time-out on some balls and schedule them on the calendar, so you will not forget to hit them later.

The same goes for those emails. First, unsubscribe from all the silly distributions you do not need and never read. You would not ask your tennis opponent to serve extra balls all at once that are not part of the game. As the real balls come in, either answer them, file them, forward them, or delete them. All four of those options take them to a different court, not yours. There will still be a few big ones left that take time, but now they are not cluttered by all the other balls and improve your focus. And as you finish the day, make sure you address every ball and clean out the inbox. You would not leave four cans of Wilson U.S. Open Tennis Balls on the court at the end of the game.

Writing this chapter was my rubber ball for the day, and it is no longer in my court. For my next tattoo, I am thinking about representing tennis. Maybe hitting the ball for match point.

Frank Lloyd Wright was mentored by Louis Sullivan who coined the term of this chapter. Wright expanded on his mentor's philosophy, *"Wright never rejects Sullivan's idea; he suggests that Sullivan didn't go far enough intellectually and spiritually. 'Less is only more where more is no good,' Wright wrote. "'Form follows function' is mere dogma until you realize the higher truth that form, and function are one.'"*[86]

Form follows function and once you have mastered that, they become one.

###

---

[86] *"The Meaning of Form follows Function,"* ThoughtCo

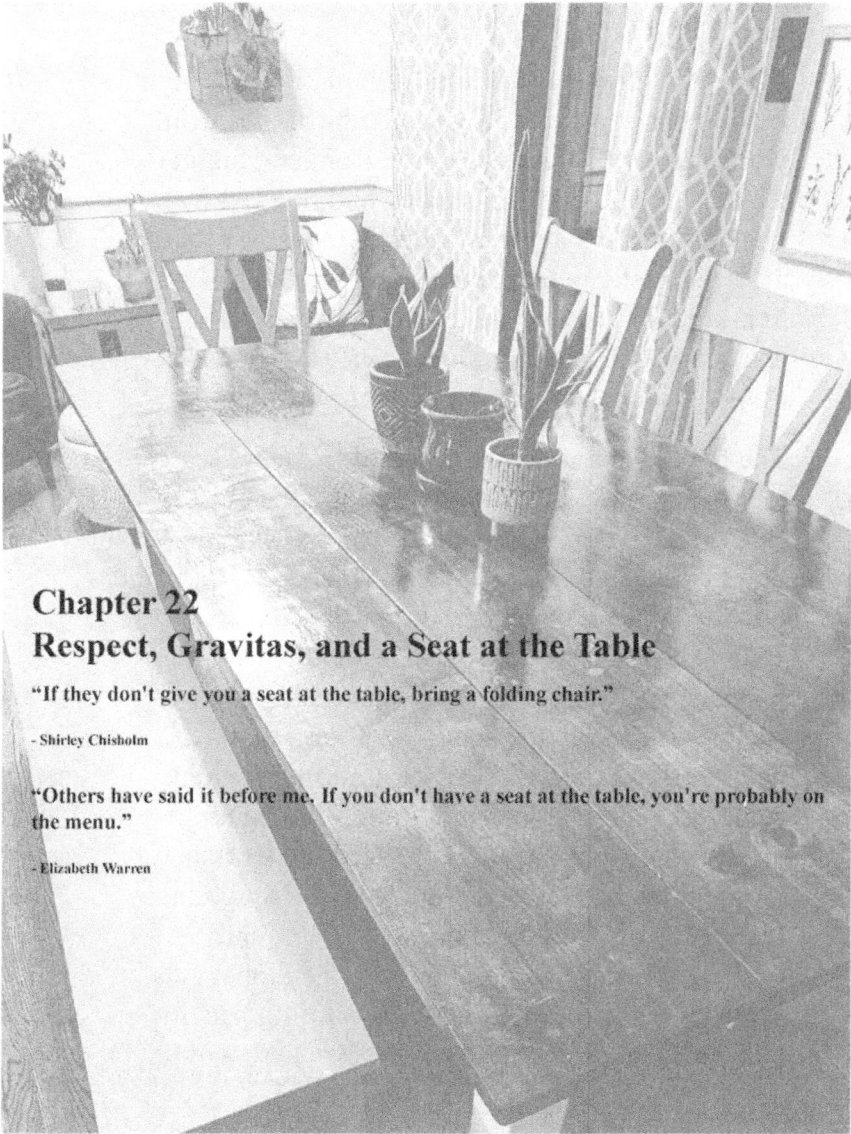

Chapter 22
Respect, Gravitas, and a Seat at the Table

"If they don't give you a seat at the table, bring a folding chair."

- Shirley Chisholm

"Others have said it before me. If you don't have a seat at the table, you're probably on the menu."

- Elizabeth Warren

Chapter 22   Respect, Gravitas, and a Scat at the Table by Dan Stoneking

My son is grown and has his own family and now I am in chapter two of my life with two beautiful young daughters. One day, my younger daughter Chloe came home from school, and boasted with glee, "Dad, I am a bucket filler!" I was so proud. after giving her a hug and a high-five, I then had to ask her exactly, what is a bucket filler? Her teacher was inspired by the book, "Have You Filled a Bucket Today?" by Carol McCloud.[87]

The book explains that when you are being kind to yourself and others, you are filling the bucket. But when you are being mean, you are dipping into that bucket. My daughter's teacher expanded on the theme and included things like respect, responsibility on the filling side and their opposites on the dipping side. It struck me as such a simple but powerful illustration that the next morning I expanded it even further with my team of twenty and included things like making deadlines, inspired teamwork, accurate work and more on the bucket filler side, while listing things like being late, missing those deadlines, and receiving customer complaints on the dipper side. We actually had some fun brainstorming lists for both sides. Over the next few weeks there would

---

[87] *"Have You Filled a Bucket Today,"* Amazon

be jokes about people's actions and whether they were a filler or a dipper. At the simplest level, all anyone needs to do to earn a seat at the table is to be a bucket filler. But life is not always that simple.

30,000 Feet

Respect, Gravitas, and a Seat at the Table

These qualities are not synonyms, but rather they are overlapping and complementary. *If you respect someone* it means that you admire them deeply, as a result of their abilities, qualities, or achievements. These can cover a wide array of characteristics and do not need to be all inclusive. In fact, they seldom are. I respect Olympic swimmer Michael Phelps for his accomplishments in the pool. I know little else about him. I respect Keanu Reeves for how naturally nice he appears in all company. I only like half of his movies. Earning respect is an essential component of reputation management, but alone, it is not enough to ensure you are fully integrated into the inner sanctum of decision-making and influence.

If you say that someone has gravitas, you mean that you respect them *because* they seem serious and intelligent. Respecting them in other ways is still great, but being seen as serious and intelligent are specific characteristics that will make people listen to you and even follow you. People who never speak up do not earn gravitas. People who do not have the right priorities or focus will not be seen with gravitas.

To have a seat at the table means that the individual has the same opportunities as everyone else to listen, share, define and influence and without retribution. Unfortunately, even if you have respect and gravitas, you still may not have a seat at the table. It could be due to perceptions of your predecessor, a lack of appreciation for communications in general, or simply a lack of consideration. The trick is to earn deep respect, develop revered gravitas and parlay them into that seat.

During the last 25 years I have had countless Public Relations, Public Information, and Public Affairs professionals complain to me about some version of them not being listened to, not being appreciated, and simply not having a seat at the table. What they did not realize was that it was always within their control to change that.

Three Feet

For those still engaged in this challenge, here are six things you can do to get that seat.

1. ***Know your stuff.*** This should be the easiest step. Nobody in your organization

knows more about what you do than you. Show them. Speak up. Enter your outreach campaigns for awards. If it helps, hang your diploma and awards in your office. Consider joining the Public Relations Society of America (PRSA) and work to get accredited through them and certified in multiple programs. Join other associations that heighten your gravitas. Take positions in those organizations. Keep up with professional reading, books, and articles, and leave copies on your desk.

2. ***Know their stuff.*** This is the first and biggest mistake communicators make. They do not take the time and energy to learn about the roles, missions and priorities of their program and operations counterparts. Granted, you will never know as much as them, but showing an effort earns respect and a long-term commitment makes your job and their job easier. If you have ever traveled to another country, you know that they appreciate even an effort at speaking their language. Same here. This dedication also builds relationships. They cannot respect you if they do not know you.

3. ***Wake up first.*** Some of you may not like hearing this one, but it is true. The most successful communicators wake up and report to work before the rest of the leadership team, especially the boss and especially during a crisis. Imagine a breaking crisis or a shocking news article in the paper. Who do you want the boss to hear from first? By being up early you not only learn about things first, and can share them, but you can also share your plan of action to respond in that same correspondence before being asked. Then get a second cup of coffee.

4. ***Demonstrate communication successes.*** If you want the seat, it is not the time to be humble. People need to see and know your accomplishments. I try to bring something to every meeting, especially the daily meeting during a crisis. And it can be done quickly. Some real examples I have shared in meetings include the White House retweeting us, information we got to a farm so they could move (and save) their livestock before a flood came in, getting messaging on the Goodyear Blimp and on the Times Square jumbotron, and getting "Homeland Security Today" to agree to run a feature

article on our work with State Emergency Managers. Remember, the litmus test for success are these things that meet all three criteria of being meaningful, measurable, and visible. Even if your success only qualifies in one, it may still be great, but if you can find examples that meet all three, it is a winner for sure. You have successes. The more the team knows about them, the more they want you included.

5. ***Provide Critical Feedback and Counsel.*** On those occasions you do get a seat, or even an understanding ear, it is finally your opportunity to leverage your ability to listen, share, define and influence. Use that ability. I have found that people often struggle in a meeting on how much, how little, or when to speak. Pretend you are in an hour-long meeting with a dozen members of the leadership team. A good rule of thumb is that if you do not speak at all, you are wrong. Conversely, if you speak the most, you are also likely wrong. That does not mean just speak for the sake of speaking or weighing in on issues of little importance. But if you are listening closely and have committed to knowing your stuff and their stuff, there

will always be a moment where you have a thought or opinion that no one else at the table has yet considered or addressed. Do it. Just pick your battles wisely, do not insult other colleagues, but offer kind, diplomatic, and purposeful input that can add value to the outcome.

6. *Passion.* I have spent my life trying to find a passion. I have tried painting, biking, writing, running, crafts, furniture building, cooking, and more. But I never felt so strongly about any of them to wake up every day wanting to do them. A few years ago, I was lamenting about this to a friend, and she seemed surprised and observed, "Dan you may or may not have 'a' passion, but you are an extremely passionate person." I learned that you can be passionate without having a passion. Be passionate about your work. It is contagious. I would like to sit at a table with you.

And while you are working on that, if you have any ideas for another passion I should try, let me know. I am hard at work on my bucket list.

###

Chapter 23 Metrics and Measurements

"Metrics are like a course in a meal. They should satisfy the need or want for something."

- Derek Huether

Chapter 23   Metrics and Measurements by
Dan Stoneking *and* Rebecca Kuperberg

In this chapter we decided to do a kind of *He
Said / She Said* or *Point / Counterpoint* approach.
You may or may not have specific requirements.
You may or may not have the authority to make
change. But hopefully, you agree that crisis
communications is both an art and a science. And
we thought you would best be served by two
different perspectives.

AITA? by Dan Stoneking

If you are not familiar with the acronyms, I will
share a brief primer. The social media website
Reddit has a popular subreddit section where
people share incidents and moments from their
lives and then ask complete strangers Am I The
A$$hole (AITA)?[88] Subscribers then pronounce
their judgements, take sides, and declare their
opinions. I do not subscribe to Reddit, but this
has become so popular that I discovered months
ago (okay, years ago) that it pops up in other
feeds and social media that I follow. I mean, the
dark side algorithm will not let me escape it. And
I am fine with that. I like peeking behind the
curtain to see what absurd things people do and
fight about. And, like millions of others, I like to

---

[88] *Am I the Asshole?* Reddit

pass judgment. I have never written a reply since I do not subscribe, but I have had great conversations and a few serious judgments in my head.

Recently, I came to an epiphany of sorts. People do not agree on human behavior. People often do not even know why others or even themselves behave the way they do. The disagreement prompts the original post and then thousands of others go on to pass judgment and take sides or accept/reject both sides. That is at least four different opinions on one behavior. And here is where I segue to crisis communications and metrics.

Why do we message the media and the public during a crisis? To educate? Inform? Motivate action? Yes, to all of that. But at the foundation, aren't we trying to change behavior? We want people to evacuate or stay indoors or help a neighbor. We want the media to promote that our agency is doing a respectable job or to show a video of us doing meaningful work while we wear our branded clothing. All of that is behavior change.

And somewhere in this process the boss comes to the crisis communicator and says something to the effect of "I would like to see metrics on the effectiveness of our outreach." They want to know if we are changing behavior.

So, how do we measure our outreach? Quantitative data is numbers-based and easily measurable. For example, how many releases we published, how many social media posts, and the number of interviews conducted. Extremely easy to do, but none of these address behavior change. Qualitative data is more interpretation based and can help us understand why, how, or what happened behind certain behaviors. What did people say in interviews or focus groups? What were the common patterns or themes? Are these specific to those people or can they be generalized to the wider group? That would be immensely helpful. However, for most organizations it is impossible to accomplish. There are academic behavioral studies that take years of research to accomplish.

Quantitative is easy but meaningless. Qualitative is meaningful, but exceedingly difficult. Say it with me - Quantitative is easy but meaningless. Qualitative is meaningful, but exceedingly difficult.

Let us take an example or two in a crisis situation. Let us assume more people evacuated a community than during a previous storm or more people bought flood insurance this year. Both wonderful things. Both are measurable. Both are qualitative since people made choices, changed their behavior and acted differently than prior. But here is the rub. How can anyone measurably prove that those changes were the result of an agency news release, a social media post, or a video that aired on NBC News? We cannot. People are more complicated than that. Maybe their neighbor convinced them to change. Maybe people had more valuables to protect. Maybe some folks just had a little more spare savings. Maybe it is simple experiential learning because they paid a price for not evacuating or having flood insurance before.

Can you imagine going to a boss and convincing them their direction for metrics might be misguided and more complicated than they understand? Not an easy conversation to have. I have tried. So, what most people tend to do in crisis communications is pacify the requests and make attractive reports on quantitative and qualitative data that are indefensible but seem to appease.

I would like to suggest another option - we all fight the good fight and educate internal audiences and leadership that crisis communications are both a science and an art. Intuition matters. Instincts matter. Throwing things on the wall and trying them out matters.

We are that round object that decision-makers want to put into the square box that the logisticians and planners work in. We do not need to apologize for being different. We should embrace it.

I think we should stand up firmly and proudly and push back on meaningless metrics. And if that fails, I guess we can pose our problem to strangers on Reddit.

###

Agree to Disagree or Agree to Agree? By Rebecca Kuperberg

I agree. Well, kind of. I will start with some background, move to where I agree with Dan, then share where I disagree, and finally I will offer a place where we might be able to find common ground despite our differences.

I will start by saying that this conversation is important. "Data" has exploded over the last twenty years. Our decisions, particularly our decisions online, have become data points that computer scientists, machine learning experts, and data scientists can access. When we open an email, that is a datapoint. When we open the attachment or click on a link, we generate other data points. When we go to a news site and click on one story but not another, these decisions yield multiple data points. Even how fast we click a link, or how fast we move on from a webpage- these too are data points. According to a Forbes article,[89] in 2018 we created 2.5 quintillion bytes of data every day. Every year, that number goes up by about 23%. By 2024, it is estimated that we will generate 147 zettabytes of data in a year. In case that measure sounds alien to you too, one zettabyte is equal to a trillion gigabytes.

Interest in data-driven decision making has also expanded as more data is being generated and more data is accessible. I do not see data and metrics becoming less significant or less important in the coming years (or coming decades for that matter).

Not only is this conversation important, but we are also far from the only people disagreeing about how and when data should be used. To this day, there are many people who argue that academic findings, or solutions to problems, are only legitimate if they are backed up by quantitative data or statistics. On the other side, there are those who argue that only qualitative data can actually tell us that X causes Y, as Dan described above. More recently, there are a growing number of experts in the middle. Those

---

[89] *How Much Data do we Create Everyday,* Forbes

who argue that both forms of data are meaningful, depending on context, and can be complementary, used together to develop even stronger arguments.

Agree: I agree with Dan that we need to push back on meaningless metrics. Collecting data for the sake of collecting data is not helping anyone. And while it can *sound* impressive to say, "our email had an 87% open rate," we need to understand what that means and why it matters, if it even does.

Disagree: I disagree with Dan's mantra that quantitative is easy but meaningless and qualitative is meaningful but exceedingly difficult. They both are, or least they can be, challenging. And they can both be meaningful or meaningless.

Instead, I will offer a perspective that is less catchy. It is easy to collect easy-to-collect data. Sometimes, data that is easy to collect answers a question that matters to us. For example, an easy datapoint to measure and collect is how many "likes" a social media post receives. We can all go on to our social media platform of choice, look at a post, and see how many likes it got. We can look at 10 posts and make a small spreadsheet with the post, the author, the date, and the number of likes. It does not even need to be in Excel- we can write it in a notebook.

Let us say our question is: which post is receiving the most attention? Likes are not a perfect measure. A post may get fewer likes but more "shares" (but we can add those to our spreadsheet too). Maybe a post is being viewed by many people, but they are not interacting with it. It depends how we define attention. Ultimately, likes, shares, even views are not perfect measures, but they can help us answer our question. But that question is not that exciting. Why do we care if a post gets attention? Perhaps we care if a post is effective, if people read the information, digest it, and change their behavior or opinion because of it. If our question is: which post is most effective? Likes are not going to answer that question for us. We may not be able to ever answer that question confidently but could get closer to understanding it through other data, including qualitative data.

For me, qualitative is neither more meaningful nor more important than quantitative data. Rather, there are two things that matter more: focusing on the question and how it is best answered and making sure that data is valid, meaning that it measures what we want it to measure.

Focusing on the question: As a (former) political scientist, I was taught that we need to do problem-driven research. With the data explosion that I mentioned above, scholars were taking existing data, fitting it into a formula, and then essentially drafting a paper backwards- start with the conclusion and then think about why it matters and what types of questions it might answer. Rinse, repeat with a new variable or new dataset. If you think that sounds boring, you would be right.

This drove a new call for political science and for similar academic disciplines: we need to get back to problem-driven research. Rather than start with the conclusion, our work needs to be motivated by real and big problems. And there are, unfortunately, many. Those problems generate important questions. In emergency management, we might ask: why do people rebuild in a flood zone when they could relocate elsewhere? Why are some people less willing to go to safety when a wildfire is approaching? Is it possible, or desirable, to separate vulnerability before a disaster from vulnerability during and after?

These are big questions. And they are not easily answerable. But they are the important questions. And even if we can only chip away at the answers with the data we have right now, over time we can expand on those answers and improve outcomes. It is more important to answer a small piece of an important question than to fully answer an unimportant question.

Measuring what we want to measure: Data also needs to be valid. We should accurately measure what we want to measure. This gets at the data itself, but also how we collect and use it. Let us say we have the home phone numbers of everyone in a town and call to ask them if they have an emergency plan. We might assume that we can take those results and have a good sense of what proportion of the town has an emergency plan, right? Maybe.

First, how many people answered their phones? Second, is it possible that we worded the question in such a way that people may misinterpret the question or be dishonest because they do not want to admit they do not have a plan? Finally, how many households do not have a home phone number at all?

This last point is particularly relevant as we think about underserved communities. When data is biased, because it undercounts or undervalues a group of people, it may not be valid. These biases are not usually intentional. But whether intentional or not, when invalid or biased data is used to make broader claims, it can exacerbate vulnerabilities. If younger, older, or poorer community members are routinely left out of data-driven decisions, their needs are less likely to be met.

Just because data can be large and abstract, it does not mean that it is flawless or objective. To combat these challenges, we need to bring different people into the conversation, look critically at data, and not overgeneralize our findings. We also have to remember that abstract data are still connected to individuals. People, with our limitations and our biases, for worse and for better, are at the heart of data.

###

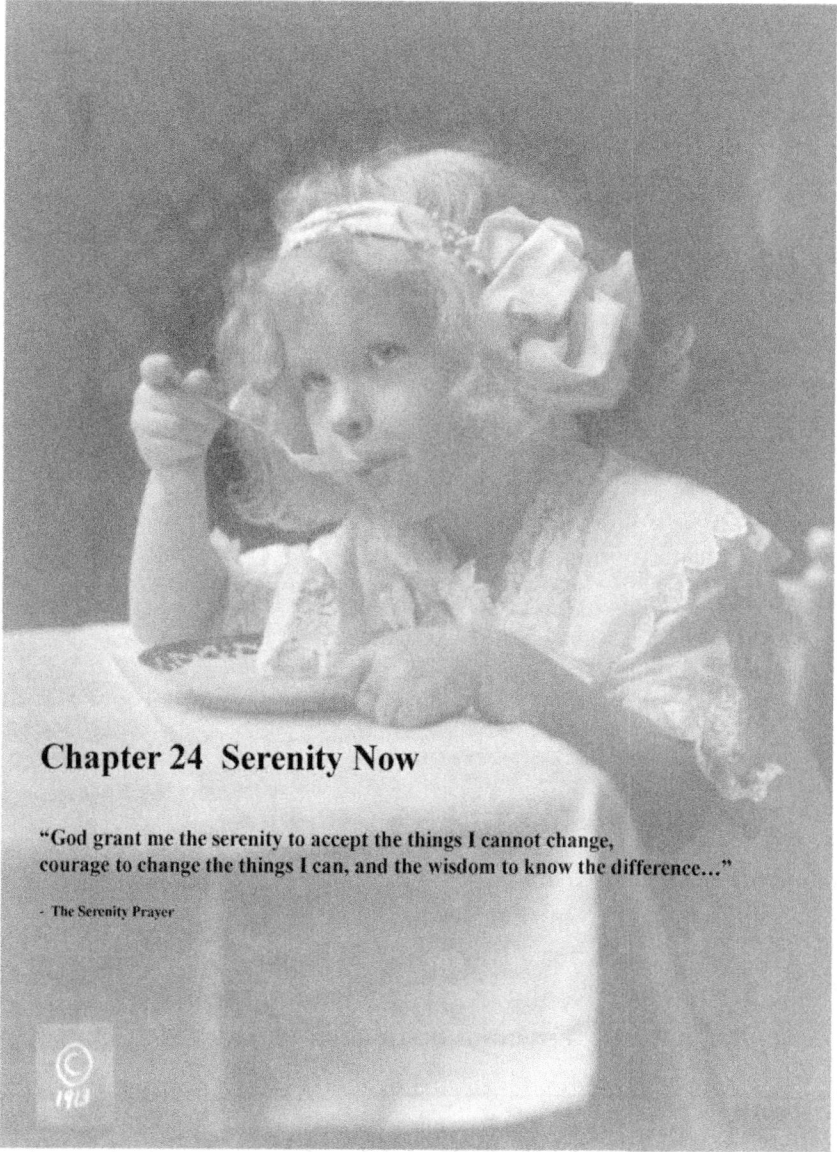

Chapter 24 Serenity Now

"God grant me the serenity to accept the things I cannot change,
courage to change the things I can, and the wisdom to know the difference..."

- The Serenity Prayer

Chapter 24 Serenity Now by Dan Stoneking

In the television show, "Seinfeld," the character Frank Costanza (played brilliantly by Jerry Stiller), in order to keep his stress and blood pressure down, will occasionally proclaim, "Serenity now!"[90] I wish it were that easy. It is not.

Abraham Mazlow captured our needs better in a methodical progression to serenity, aptly called *Maslow's Hierarchy Of Needs.*[91] I will trust that all of you have navigated your way through psychological needs, safety needs, love and understanding. If you have not, I am afraid that I cannot help you, especially with only a few chapters to go. But I do want to take a moment to address Esteem and Self-Actualization based on my 35+ years' experience as a crisis communicator and my 60+ years on the planet. Maybe something will resonate with you.

30,000 Feet (Esteem)

Esteem results from earning a level of respect, status, and recognition. I will boast enough bravado to comfortably claim that I have achieved this. Do not worry, my humility will come in the next section. If you are still striving

---

[90] *"The Serenity Now Episode,"* IMDb
[91] *"Mazlow's Hierarchy of Needs,"* Simply Psychology

to achieve, improve, or refine your level of esteem, then I suggest that you are never too young to have a bucket list.

I recently retired from full time federal government work and started my bucket list. It is fun. I recently set a personal record by riding my bike for more than fifty miles. That was on my list. I authored a book of poems. Soon, I am going on a ride in a hot-air balloon for the first time. The week after that I will enter my first mud run. And, hopefully, by the time you read this, I will have made reservations at Hell's Kitchen in Washington, DC to try Beef Wellington for the first time. All of these are bucket list items.

Which begs the question, why was I waiting? They say that "youth is wasted on the young." I think the counter to that is that bucket lists are wasted by only going to the old. More than that, why don't we hear about bucket lists for our jobs?

When I was working in my last position, I had a reputation for often stating a few mantras, like "Let's make a difference on the planet" and "If I were king for a day…." But, looking back, we were kings, and we did make a difference on the planet. Sometimes it was a target of opportunity. Other times the result of necessity. On a few occasions, we took time to brainstorm. But if I had to do it all over again, I think I would gather the team to make a crisis communications bucket list. I encourage you to do it before it is too late. Writing things down tends to result in greater accomplishments. And if you brainstorm with a team and post your bucket list for all to see, the accountability will motivate you even more to that lofty level of esteem.

If I had to do it all over again, here are a few things that I would include. Feel free to borrow, steal, adapt, add-on, and surpass any level of crisis communications esteem I could not even dream to attain. And if you only accomplish a few of these, or your own bucket list, I promise they will bring you a level of serenity.

- Spend less time on budgets, forms and reports and more time engaging stakeholders
- Put innovation over stagnation
- Less time with computers and more time with people
- Do fun things that make you laugh
- Establish work hours for required professional development reading
- Spend a day far away from the office, taking pictures, finding emotion through imagery

- Change the paradigm on risk communications to one of self-reliance
- Sit down with more survivors and listen to their stories
- Have lunch once a week with a different team member
- Deploy to more disasters or crises to help others and learn more
- Persuade internal colleagues upon the value proposition of crisis communications
- Challenge every member of the team to produce a compelling and persuasive video
- Turn the adversity between local, state, and federal responders into collaboration
- Avoid the consistency of relying on the same social media platforms every time, when they do not suffice for all events and audiences
- Invest more in engaging younger people in preparedness
- Attend town halls and community events before disasters occur
- Bypass the boring template news releases in favor of compelling human-interest stories
- Make websites that meet the needs of survivors, not ones limited by weak platforms

- Get crisis communicators to serve details at various levels of different organizations
- Establish formal organizational training on how to be a storyteller
- Schedule one hour a week with the team with no other agenda than brainstorming
- Make technology serve the mission, not the mission serving technology

I could go on and triple this list easily. So could you. The bucket list is the beginning. Checking them off, well, that is the ticket right there.

And here is the real beauty. Bucket lists can be endless. I still have not found time to get a motorcycle license so I can ride a Harley Davidson. I have not yet made Jambalaya from scratch. I have not performed a stand-up comedy act. And I have never been to Wyoming. But they are on the list. And I will.

Three Feet (Self-Actualization)

I promised humility. Here it is. I do not know if I am self-actualized. Probably not. I am still a work in progress. It is a journey, not a destination. Maybe it will help if I share this true story from my life.

I was seventeen years old the first time I swore at my dad. I was seventeen-years old the last time I swore at my dad. It was one of my first jobs. At the end of each summer, we would disassemble and take docks out of Lake Winnipesaukee, to prevent damage from the lake icing up each winter. And then each May or June we would return to put them back in the water. On this particularly hot June morning, we approached a new job. It was a massive and heavy dock that for some reason had been moved more than forty feet from the shore the season before. It could not be lifted, not by the two of us, so we attempted to dig in our feet and push. It moved about six inches.

"Again," my Dad shouted. Maybe five inches. It seemed like my Dad's voice got louder and angrier the less the dock moved. The fifth time that he yelled at me, it sparked some inner teenage testosterone that I could not control.

"*You* F&#$'ing move it," I shouted boldly, and I turned and walked away. I was done. This was not my fault nor my problem. I walked out the driveway and took a right on Bean Road, about six miles from our home. I walked for about a mile and a half, convincing myself that my Dad was unreasonable and giving me a tough time for his problem. At the same time, the heat was bearing down on me, and I slowly came to the realization that our home was still a long walk away, and if I did keep going, I would just have to wait that much longer for my punishment. The heat also evaporated much of my testosterone, anger, and courage. I reluctantly turned around and slowly started my way back. As I hit the driveway, I was almost shaking at the thought of how angry he would be when I turned the corner of the house. He did not see me at first. The dock was no longer forty feet from the water. It was a mere four feet away. He barely looked over his shoulder as I walked nearer.

"If we just keep pushing...," he said with a quiet determination as he dug his feet into the ground without finishing his sentence. I quickly got in position beside him and dug deeper and pushed harder than I could before. In less than a few minutes the dock was in the water, and we were fastening bolts and pipes to complete the assembly. We finished the job in silence until we walked toward the pick-up truck.

Dad put his arm around my shoulder and quietly suggested as he looked ahead, not at me, "let's head on home and see if your Mom has any iced tea waiting for us."

Just keep pushing. That is something all of us can do, every day at work. Have a difficult day? Wake up tomorrow and keep pushing. Try to achieve something every day that you want to go home and tell someone about. No achievement today? It is okay, just keep pushing, and follow your serenity every day. Acceptance. Courage. Wisdom.

Three Inches

Wow. Look. This section was not in the other chapters. That is how important serenity is. If 30,000 feet is the strategic view, and three feet is the operational/tactical view, then what is three inches? Introspection. You read this book because you are interested in crisis communications. You wanted to find a few tips and tricks that will make you better. That is great. That is why we wrote it. But there is more to life. In a world where everyone wants you to do more and better, you can. But you do not have to do more and better. Certainly not every day. And you do not have to feel bad if you do not do more and better. That is self-actualization. One of my favorite Billy Joel songs, "The Stranger,"[92] goes, in part, like this:

"Well, we all have a face
That we hide away forever
And we take them out and show ourselves
When everyone has gone
Some are satin, some are steel
Some are silk and some are leather

---

[92] *"The Stranger,"* Billy Joel azlyrics

They're the faces of the stranger
But we love to try them on"

At the beginning of this book, I said, "the beauty of art is our opportunity to interpret what we consume." My interpretation of Joel's lyrics here is that he is reminding us that there is a version of ourselves we often hide away. Embrace that person. They say you have to have a thick skin to risk rejection as an actor or a writer. That experience can pale in comparison to the life of a crisis communicator, never knowing when and what the next crisis will be and never knowing who will ask what on the next call. Serenity is essential. I worked with more than four hundred people in my last position and every one of them had skills and talents that I did not. And you have skills, talents, and ideas that others do not.

As passionate as I am about crisis communications, I value being a dad more. I am better at being a dad. And I am okay with that. My wish for you is that you revel in your experiences as a crisis communicator, but more so, I wish you serenity and peace. You are allowed to want and have that too.

###

Chapter 25 Disaster Stories

"What we've got here is failure to communicate..."

- Strother Martin
as Captain from Cool Hand Luke

"Hey, what do you say we both be independent together, huh?"

- Hermey the Dentist to Rudolph
from the movie, Rudolph the Red-Nosed Reindeer

Chapter 25   Disaster Stories by Dan Stoneking

In this last chapter, I am sharing personal thoughts and insights that I wrote either in the response phase, recovery phase, or shortly thereafter of each of the disasters. They are shared here in the chronological order they occurred. I did not write for every disaster when I deployed, but each of these four disasters left an indelible impact on me and stretched, if not completely redefined for me the humanity within disasters. I believe that many of us who work crisis communications are writers at heart as well. Journaling is a wonderful way to capture events and memories in your voice, whether for posterity, self-reflection, or something to give your grandchildren someday. These can also offer you perspective and lessons learned for the next disaster. Reflection is healthy, even cathartic at times. There may be misspellings or grammar errors because I wrote these for me. The content is what matters. I share them without edits, warts and all.

I believe everyone in our country who was alive at the time has a story about 9/11. Their own story about how it impacted them and what that day meant to them. No story is more or less important than any other story. This is just my story. I was in the Pentagon that morning.

The Pentagon (Sep 2001)

Autumn arrived quickly, and I was glad. Having arrived at my new job in the Pentagon on July 23rd, I had told my friends that I could not wait until the end of September, when, after sixty days of experience, I would have a better handle on how to be an effective Pentagon Spokesman. Here I was, ahead of schedule, shy of the sixty days, and doing well. I had already survived briefings and queries on the forest fires out West and a tragic plane crash that took the lives of 21 National Guard members. I knew my job and I felt comfortable.

That Tuesday began quietly enough. We had a regular briefing scheduled like we did every Tuesday and Thursday. My only responsibility of the day was to escort some officers of the Naval Reserve to watch our daily Press Briefing as part of their professional development. At about 8:30 a.m., I sent an email reminder to my Naval Reserve counterpart letting him know where and when I would meet the group. The TV on my desk was turned on to CNN, but muted, so I could concentrate on my emails. I yawned as I began reading our manual for duty officer procedures and tried to keep my mind from drifting off into thoughts of a scenic run along the Potomac.

"Holy S#@$," I heard one of my co-workers shout from across the Press Room.

"Channel two," another co-worker barked. It was common for us to yell out to each other and draw attention to media reports, but their intensity was disarming. I turned toward my TV and raised the volume. It was 8:46 a.m.

I watched a dark flume of smoke billowing out of some of the higher floors of one of the World Trade Center buildings. As my colleagues conjectured on the cause, I grabbed the phone and called the Command Center for a Situation Report (SITREP). One of my responsibilities was to be the Pentagon Spokesman for Disasters. This was clearly going to be in my lane. The Command Center indicated that they were faxing me the SITREP and before I could get out of my seat, Pentagon Correspondents were at my desk asking for an explanation of the event and the phone started ringing.

I gave them a preliminary briefing, checked the fax, which had not arrived yet, and began a log of events. As I continued to answer questions, while watching the TV, I picked up the phone to call the Command Center. "Where's that fax," I pressed them, "I need it two minutes ago—

"Holy F#@*," someone screamed. I turned to the TV and watched United Airlines Flight 175 crash into the second World Trade Center building. It was 9:02 a.m. Truly a moment frozen in time, so many things became instantly clear. We were being attacked. The United States of America was being attacked. We were at War. The world had changed. The first building was not an accident. There could be more. Everyone started moving. I kept the Command Center on the line as they continued to update me. Somebody was calling the Joint Chiefs of Staff office. Somebody else called the Army; and someone else, the Air Force; and still another called the New York National Guard. Every phone was either ringing or being used to call out. Everyone was talking at once. People were flipping channels, looking at different angles, trying to make sense of what had happened.

"Sir, we can't seem to get the SITREP fax to go through, and we have another classified update you need to see" the command center, still glued to my left ear, drew me away from the TV reports.

"I can't wait any longer," I responded. "I'm coming to you." I told my co-workers where I was going, and I headed for the door.

"What if they hit the Pentagon," I heard someone ask, over my shoulder, as I cleared the doorway and headed down the hallway.

"People can be so paranoid," I thought as I paced quickly down the corridor. My office was in the outer E-Ring at the end of the seventh corridor. I was heading toward an office between the 5th and 6th Corridors, still on the E-Ring. Still heading west, I was almost at my destination when I heard a loud explosion, felt the floor bounce, and saw dark smoke emanating toward me. People flew out of every door along the hallway, almost simultaneously, and started running. I would have described it as cartoonish if it were not real. It was 9:37 a.m.

There was no doubt in my mind what had occurred. I knew immediately and did an about-face to return to my office to get my marching orders. On the way back, I realized by the frenzied remarks, that most people had no idea what had happened. Not many offices have TV's on their desks. Halfway back to my office, the sirens went off and the loudspeakers directed everyone to exit the building. I ignored the directive and continued on. I arrived back at the Press Office minutes later to discover everyone had gone. I returned to the hallway and followed the cattle-like movement toward the exit.

Most people were surprisingly calm. Certainly, many of them had no idea what had happened. Those on the far side of the building may not have even heard the impact. But as we made our way slowly, occasionally I would hear someone crying or other frantic exclamations. As we rounded a corner and passed the courtyard, everyone could see and smell the smoke again. For those who were not previously aware, the fervor and urgency increased. As we finally approached the exits, the lines split in two and many left our line for the smaller one. I remained in my line. Not out of any bravado or false bravery. Actually, I was thinking about my nightly commute, and how every time I switched lanes, that lane would slow down. The thought almost made me laugh.

Then I looked up at a clock on the wall. It was 9:50 a.m. I knew what many around me did not know. I knew that the two Trade Centers were hit somewhere between 14 and 18 minutes apart. At this point, the plane had struck the Pentagon 13 minutes earlier and there were several hundred people between the door and me. Would there be another? I felt eerily resigned to my fate as I took small steps and tried to smile reassuringly to the worried faces around me.

A few minutes past ten o'clock, I was joining thousands of others in the sunshine of the parking lot. Dark smoke filtered into the sky from what used to be the fifth corridor. Sirens blared. Some people scurried. Others dialed away furiously on cell phones that were not working. Federal buildings all throughout Crystal City and Pentagon City were being evacuated. The streets were at a stand-still with vehicles and pedestrians.

I gave my business card to a co-worker I had found. I told him I was going to the National Guard Bureau office in Crystal City and would set up temporary operations there. I wrote the number on the back of my card and headed out of the parking lot, on my way. With over 40,000 people scrambling around and at least a half dozen paths between our buildings I chose a path and began weaving through the crowd. As I walked, I dialed away at my cell phone as well. After repeated tries I finally got through to my son. "I'm okay," I told him.

"Why wouldn't you be?" he mumbled back from a sleepy haze. I forgot that he had worked the night shift.

"Turn on the television," I said. I will call you again as soon as I can.

The next few hours, days and weeks became foggy. I worked the first-forty hours straight. My co-workers began shift work at a gas station in close proximity to the still smoking and smoldering Pentagon. They had one telephone and no automation. I provided the fax, computer, and internet link from my location to internal and external audiences. Once my colleagues were able to set up full operations again inside the Pentagon, I took a few hours off and went home to sleep. There were twenty-seven messages on my answering machine when I finally got there.

About two or three weeks after the attack, three tornadoes swept across D.C, one of them directly on the grounds of the Pentagon, as I was leaving work at the end of the day. I pulled the car over and watched branches falling in the street and saw one of the tornadoes edge eerily and taunting just past the Washington Monument. I later learned two sisters at the University of Maryland died from Mother Nature's assault that day.

A few weeks after that, on an evening when I was the Pentagon Public Affairs Staff Duty Officer, I got a phone call. Anthrax had been found in the Pentagon. Only three buildings in the world were attacked that fateful day. The Pentagon was one of them. Only a half a dozen buildings in the world had found Anthrax. The Pentagon was one of them. Only one building on the entire planet was attacked by a passenger plane turned into a weapon, weathered a tornado, and endured the strain of Anthrax. The Pentagon.

###

Fast forward a few years. I was working as the Deputy Director of Public Affairs at the National

Guard Bureau. We had been tracking Hurricane Katrina's approach to land. I got a call from the Chief of the Guard Bureau, LTG Steve Blum. He told me and one other officer to grab our bags and meet him at Andrews Air Force Base. We did not know at that moment that we would not be on the return flight.

Pete's Truck (Aug-Sep 2005)

Hurricane Katrina was the costliest and one of the five deadliest hurricanes in the history of the United States at its time. Katrina formed on August 23 during the 2005 Atlantic hurricane season and caused devastation along much of the north-central Gulf Coast. On August 28th, 2005, Hurricane Katrina hit the southern coast of the United States with devastating effect. It was reported that more than 1,800 people lost their lives, and more than $81 billion dollars in damages occurred. The most severe loss of life and property damage occurred in New Orleans, Louisiana. By late morning on August 29th overtopping of levees and flooding in New Orleans had begun. Within 4 hours of Hurricane Katrina's passage, Army National Guard Citizen-Soldiers were in the water saving lives. At 11:00 p.m. that evening I arrived from Washington D.C. and reported to the Emergency Operation Center (EOC) in Baton Rouge to offer help to my public affairs counterpart, Pete.

"The National Guard Bureau is here to help?" he questioned me, with particular disdain on the last word." What began with understandable tension evolved into a brotherhood over the next eleven days.

Much has been written about Hurricane Katrina with considerable finger pointing. To this day, I still lack the energy to write a definitive expose on who was right and who was wrong. In large measure, all the blame and credit mongers disillusion me. There is another story there of heroes and everyday citizens who made sacrifices to help. But I will wait for another time to address the bigger picture. For now, I simply want to touch on a few of my firsthand experiences and lessons learned specifically in the area of public affairs.

Pete and I quickly formed a bond and worked together to tell the story. As the local lead for Louisiana National Guard support, he filled the role as spokesperson and coordinator there at the Baton Rouge EOC, while I took daily UH-60A Black Hawk helicopter flights filled with a mixture of local and national reporters and television crews. Each day we would take flights through the city, providing the aerial shots they all requested, and visit Belle Chasse Naval Air Station, where National Guard troops were arriving hourly and daily to help in the response and recovery efforts. Beyond that, we would make additional stops where these troops were deploying to assist community members.

A few things continue to stand out in my mind from this experience. I will not forget the young sergeant who told me about the day he stepped into an elderly nursing home to find a few dozen senior citizens dead. He described them as appearing to have practically died in place, in beds and chairs, without having a chance to attempt escape. The sergeant went on to explain, with distant eyes not making contact with anyone in the group at the time, that what he saw in New Orleans was far worse than anything he experienced in combat. He had served a tour in Iraq the year prior.

I will not forget the day Pete and I visited Jackson Barracks, the Louisiana National Guard Headquarters where many National Guard members had to evacuate by boat from the second story before they could begin helping others. It was also where Pete's office was, and his truck was parked when the flooding occurred. The day we returned was about a week later. Most of the water had subsided. As we approached, Pete went straight to his truck. Like all of them in the parking lot it was battered pretty bad and "totaled" by insurance standards. The roof had sharp dents in it that were formed by the propeller blades of rescue boats when the truck was immersed beneath the water. Pete surveyed the situation, reached in to grab some personal belongings and then turned to me with a smile and said, "Do you want to go see what my office looks like?"

The last observation I will share may be less sensational but impacts me no less than the first two. Not only did I help the media get their aerial shots of downtown New Orleans and the Superdome and rooftops jutting barely above the waterline, but like millions of other Americans, I have seen them replayed enough on television to be jaded. Two other forgettable images are forged deeper in my conscience. One afternoon, while walking across a field more than four hundred meters from the water's edge, I saw some dead fish in the grass and smelled decay all around me. It would not translate well in a television news story. It may not translate here in print, but the sense of smell has a long memory and that one still lingers.

On another day, I took some media to St. Tammany Parish, North of New Orleans and Lake Pontchartrain. I showed them a National Guard Engineering unit removing fallen trees, branches, and debris so a local elementary school could open back up. One of the national-level media crews was unimpressed and wanted to return to New Orleans, where "the story was at." It reminded me of that allegory of the little girl who was throwing starfish back into the ocean. A man approaches her and says, "Look at how many starfish there are. You cannot throw them all back into the ocean before they die. Why are you doing this? It is not going to make a difference." And the little girl replies, as she throws another starfish back into the ocean, "It made a difference to that one." I wanted to explain that to the reporter but did not. The repairs that day may not have made a dramatic television shot, but hundreds of young people were able to return to education and some normalcy – and that is a story worth telling.

Public Affairs Lessons Learned (or reinforced)

If I had to sum the bullets below into one thought it would be this – there seems to be a certain ethos to public affairs professionals, and it needs to change. This may sound harsh, and I apologize in advance...wait for it...but I think, in general, we need to change from narcissist, sycophant, ethnocentric, verbose, self-indulgent....into strategically, tactically, technically competent, human resource-oriented, logistical, selfless, message-focused warriors.

Other lessons include:

- Public Affairs/Public Information Officers should be school trained
- We need to go where the action is, get dirty, and earn our stripes
- Command emphasis is critical
- Lack of command emphasis is not an excuse
- Organizational and administrative skills are as important as being media savvy
- Email folder management is essential
- Email distributions need to be established and updated quickly
- Need to know who is assigned where
- Schedule for updates/briefings must be consistent and announced
- Desk/laptop/phone for each individual assigned
- Personnel rotations (shifts and tours)
- Lodging (cots) and transportation
- Communications is paramount (sat phones, cells, blackberry)
- Common Operating Picture (COP) must be determined and shared
- PAO/PIO's must have an organizational structure
- Ability to improvise and adapt (as a PAO I had a dedicated helicopter)
- Access to the people and the story
- Need to understand what Media wants vs what Organization wants

- Must establish a public affairs battle rhythm
- Many PAO's prefer being on camera or writing the story, but they should also...
  - Read and know all doctrine and guidance
  - Fill personnel vacancies
  - Fill logistical shortages
  - Know how to uplink/distribute the articles, photos, videos we take
  - Respond to emails and voicemails
  - Learn how to maximize resources
  - Know the right players
- Perception vs Reality - always have to be aware of both
- PAO's need more training on media nuances
- Need both national and local coverage (not mutually exclusive)
- TV personalities increase likelihood of airtime (over film crew only)
- PAO's can/should influence what a banner or crawl will say
- Basics – Branding can and should be both visual and verbal.

National Guard Hurricane Katrina Talking Points

I drafted or contributed to most of the following:

- Guard forces were in the water and on the streets rescuing people within four hours of Katrina's passing
- The nation's governors dispatched more than 50,000 National Guard members from every state and territory to respond to Hurricane Katrina
- Rescued and evacuated more than 70,000 people from life threatening situations in the hours and days following Katrina
- The cumulative Army and Air National Guard air operations for Hurricane Katrina by 29 Sep were over 10,200 sorties flown, 88,100 passengers airlifted, 18,834 cargo tons moved, and 17,000 lives saved
- With over 50,000 National Guard personnel mobilized on 8 Sep, the Guard exceeded by three times its previous largest deployment ever for a natural disaster
- The Air National Guard's air operations for Hurricane Katrina were over 2,200 sorties flown for 7,200 flying hours, airlifting 31,200 passengers, moving 11,200 cargo tons, and saving 1,400 lives
- The National Guard helped evacuate victims from the Convention Center as fast as civilian agencies could provide bus

transportation–a rate of approximately 1,000 individuals per hour

- Stabilized Convention Center in less than 30 minutes; within 90 minutes, hot meals were served to 20,000 citizens; within 18 hours, over 20,000 evacuees were bussed out of the convention center

As I look back in years to come, the tragedy and sorrow will not fade. Nor will I ever forget the moment I saw Pete's truck.

###

You never know when and where the next disaster will hit. One Saturday in October I was excited that there was a beer fest going on within walking distance of where I lived. I bought my tickets well in advance and that late morning, I strolled down just in time for the opening. Just as I hit the entrance, my phone rang. It was my boss. "We need you to go to American Samoa. Get packed now because the flight is leaving soon."

Life Goes On Oct 2009

In the quiet bay of Pago Pago, surrounded by Pacific hills that reach to the clouds, nestled between Sadie's by the Sea restaurant and the Pago Pago Yacht Club, just next to Samoana High School, rests the unassuming Rex H. Lee

Auditorium. The students saunter by wearing their light blue traditional lava lava school uniforms. Lunch goers stroll out from a satisfying midday meal at Sadie's and island buses pick-up and drop-off customers at the Yacht Club bus stand, exchanging pleasantries. The yacht club is unique in its charm as it has no yachts but rather lines the shore with island outrigger canoes.

In the middle of the gentle bustle of the day, on any other day, the auditorium would boast local dances and concerts, where the songs would echo out the bay.

But it is not any other day. Today, the auditorium has been converted to a Disaster Recovery Center. They come together out of necessity. They come together to recover. They have become one community, and everyone has a story. They are strong and resilient people. It is kindness and compassion that reign.

Ben works for the Small Business Administration. He tells me about the Teen Challenge Program and the cable television program he participated in to discuss the disaster and recovery programs with local teens. Ben is accustomed to speaking to national media and reaching thousands of viewers in short sound bites. On this evening, Ben and some of his federal partners invested several hours to reach a few hundred. It is a different community and a worthwhile investment. The children made food and delivered a stirring Samoan Teen Gospel show on the same program. They sang songs of thankfulness and love. I asked Ben why he did this job. The normally eloquent and effusive spokesperson tilted his head, thought for a moment, shrugged and said, "It feels good."

Bob works for the American Red Cross. He was eager to share his story about attending a memorial service at a grammar school where students and families gathered to recognize the passing of one of their classmates who lost her life in the tsunami. Bob took off his glasses and wiped his brow as he shared with me what the teacher told the gathered mourners. He said "She was talking about celebrating the life of the young girl. She talked about how she was now free. And then she explained to her students that their classmate had returned to the earth." At that precise moment in the ceremony, in the background of the service, a whale leapt from the sea. Everyone saw. No one said a word.

Typically, reporters tell other people's stories. Today, I met Mike. He is a reporter for Voice of America. Like me, he is living with a local family while on the island. He told me his story. He complimented the cute kittens in the home where he is staying. The response startled the seasoned reporter. "They weren't our kittens before the tsunami," his host told him. "But they washed up at our home and they are part of our family now."

Everyone has a story. When you ask enough questions people start asking you – did you hear the one…? I was told I need to meet Glen. Glen works for FEMA and came to American Samoa from Washington to help. His sister-in-law, Vai, lives in the village of Tula. He called when he arrived on the island and was relieved to find that she was okay. But Glen had work to do and he got right to it, establishing communications and doing his part to help communities wake up each day to a better world. So it was not until this day, today, when Vai arrived with her village at the Disaster Recovery Center that they finally got to see each other and embrace. As I type this, I am looking across the auditorium and I can see them catching up. He has his arm around her shoulder, and they are smiling. I asked him earlier what it was like – doing this kind of job for a living and having it cross over into your personal life. "I volunteered in 1970," he reflected. "To come back," he paused. "Forty years later and be able to help," another pause as he searched for the right word, and began to choke up, struggling a bit with his emotions. "It makes you feel…lucky."

A story of stories would not be complete without adding that of Moana. She shared with me a tragic version of "it was the best of times; it was the worst of times." Moana spoke slowly, as if her selfless manners made her concerned for me and whether I could keep up in my notetaking. She said, with a mother-like compassion in her soft brown eyes, that there were several casualties in Leone Village, where she is from. She described how after the tsunami passed one-half of the village was fine and spared, but the other half was shattered and most of the homes were either damaged or destroyed. "But it's only one village," she said carefully, this time looking into my eyes to make sure I understood. We sat for a while as she relayed stories among the village. She talked about how the families without homes stayed at the families with homes who shared their clothes and food. Moana spoke with pride when she told me how the people of American Samoa responded to another tsunami warning just yesterday afternoon. "I have never seen my people so alert. I am so proud of them. It is a wake-up call." I did not have any more questions, but as I thanked her and began to excuse myself, ever the polite and kind American Samoan, Moana reached out and touched my arm, "We appreciate all the help we are getting." I smiled, not knowing what to say. She was the stronger one. "Life goes on," she reassured me.

Everyone has a story in this community of communities. They are all different. They are not stories of consistency. They are stories of self-reliance. They are the stories of Ben, Bob, Mike, Glen, Vai, Moana, and some incredibly lucky kittens.

###

In early 2010, I deployed to Haiti. It was interesting because it was outside of FEMA's mission, but it was also bookmarked by two important life events from. I was finishing up my role as Acting Director and Deputy Director of Public Affairs for FEMA and would be starting in my new role as Director of Private Sector for FEMA after the deployment. In addition, right before I deployed, I gave the hospital a sperm sample because my wife and I were trying to have a baby through IVF. Upon my return, I learned we were successful and would be having a baby girl.

Life is Like a Tree January 2010

I am sitting in a cubicle in the U.S. Embassy in Port-au-Prince, Haiti. Many ceiling tiles are missing or hanging down, with lights and cables dangling among them. The paintings on the walls are cracked, broken or askew. And each cubicle is littered with files and folders that scattered upon the January 12 earthquake's impact. This cubicle belongs to Stephane. It is likely that I will never meet her. She evacuated. But from a quick glance across her work area, I can see that she has been recognized often for her service and she is clearly a woman of faith. Still pinned upon her cubicle wall is this quote, written across a background photograph of a Mapou tree:

"Life to me is like a tree, if it doesn't take its time to bloom during spring, it'll be too late in fall… there will only be the trunk and the branches left…." – Dominique M. H. Franck Jean, 1992

Haiti forests are disappearing at an enormous rate each year. The Haitians are investing in their trees. They are investing in themselves. FEMA does the same thing when we deploy to disasters. Only through deploying can we bloom, like the tree, and become true emergency managers. Each deployment offers so many opportunities to gain experience and grow.

Those who do not deploy will never meet the likes of Jim, Sarla and Rick. They were rescued together from the rubble that once was the Montana Hotel. When I met them, Jim was wearing bandages on his head and both hands. Sarla still had debris tangled in her hair. Rick walked out of the gap formed by the rescuers without a scratch. A friend of theirs from the same rescue rested nearby on a stretcher with urgent doctor care around the clock as they awaited evacuation.

I know at least two individuals who were trapped that sadly had to have a limb amputated in order to be freed. I saw the man who lost his leg. Later, I watched on the flight line while rescuers, doctors, and a pilot argued over the fate of a man nearby on his stretcher suffering from burns to 50% of his body and the further misfortune to have lost his identification. His brother negotiated on his behalf. They decided to transport him by truck to the Dominican Republic. A day after that I met Netty who told me about her good friend who was trapped. Netty texted back and forth with her for a couple of days as responders struggled through mountains of concrete to reach her. By the second day her friend's cell phone died. Soon after, so did her friend. "They kept working hard though," she told me. "At least her family will get her body back."

From every tragedy, and every deployment, there is hope. I heard one search and rescue team labored for 17 hours and got the survivor out alive. The next day another went 24 hours straight and achieved the same reward. And on the fifth day after the earthquake shook the city, one of the rescue teams found and saved a three-year-old little girl.

Each deployment brings its own unique logistical challenges as well. I forgot a razor. So, I am growing a beard. There is one shower for more than a thousand responders. I am putting the shower wipes my wife gave me to effective use. I did not have a sleeping bag so on the third day I stopped by Fairfax County Task Force Urban Search and Rescue and talked to the guys who flew in with me. They hooked me up.

There is also a quite common experience in each disaster of gradually regaining communications. Those who have not deployed really cannot have a full appreciation of that experience. Those who have deployed know what it is like for someone in Washington D.C. to question their progress even when they felt like the Lone Ranger, doing seven jobs and all without even a semaphore flag to communicate. This disaster was no different. For the first 12 hours I lugged around an emergency communication kit that took 20 minutes to set up each time in the blazing sun at the only outdoor outlet 250 yards away from the operations center, so I could provide status updates to headquarters. So, when I got text messaging to work, the AT&T technician became my new best friend and I felt like I could accomplish anything. When email started working the next day it was like a birthday present. The only drawback there is that routine work emails keep coming right along with the disaster ones. This morning my blackberry phone rang. At first, I did not recognize what that strange sound was. Of course, an hour later the phone stopped working again, but I know it will be back tomorrow. And we will keep getting faster at getting things done.

Coordination can be messy in the field. Some folks are survivors at the same time as being responders, some are territorial, and some are tired. I am learning the value of relationships. When you come across someone you met in a previous disaster, the process speeds up. Lacey and I met and worked together in American Samoa. Mark and I worked Hurricane Ike last year in Houston. There is a bond. Still, this one is different. We all began four weeks' worth of malaria pills and updated our shots. Another challenge here is getting from the embassy to the airport and back. The motor pool is stretched too thin. Darryl and I hitched a ride on the back of a truck on one trip holding on to the cargo straps that tied down 11,000 pounds of supplies as we careened down poorly paved streets. Probably will not do that again. There are several agencies from around the world. I know I will see some of them again one day. And we will coordinate better.

But the main reason everyone should deploy is to bloom during spring. To experience the humanity and the spirit to overcome that only comes when you toil side-by-side and meet the survivors we serve face-to-face. Like Bea. She works at the embassy. She is a survivor. Her mom made a rice dish for us to share, and every evening Bea makes sure we have coffee ready for the next morning. She smiles most of the time. Then there is the woman with braided hair (I wish I knew her name) who brought us all a tray of fresh papaya and pineapple. Each piece was sliced with care and decoratively displayed on a doily centered in the platter.

One of the guys here, Mervyn, lost his home. So, his chocolate brown Labrador, Bruno, stays in the storage closet at night. In the morning, he is our alarm clock. I have the morning shift walking Bruno. He has a lot of energy. I do not think anyone told him about the earthquake. He wants to play.

Today we had a memorial service. It added some hopeful solemnity that we came together to share that on Martin Luther King Day, survivors and responders alike. The Chaplain quotes from Ecclesiastes. "To every thing there is a season, and a time to every purpose under the heaven: A time to be born, and a time to die; a time to plant, and a time to pluck up that which is planted; A time to kill, and a time to heal; a time to break down, and a time to build up; A time to weep, and a time to laugh; a time to mourn…." This was our moment to mourn. Together we will heal, and we will build up. We finished the service by singing Amazing Grace together. And that is when most people cried. That is when strangers hugged. And then we returned to the business of recovery.

Everyone in FEMA should wear the FEMA blue and deploy… to experience the tragedy, logistics, coordination, and humanity. If we do not take that time to bloom, it will be too late, and we will only be left with branches.

###

When your next crisis occurs, take time for reflection. Take time to write. Capture the moment.

###

Conclusion

"The secret of being a bore... is to tell everything." - Voltaire

"Le mieux est l'ennemi du bien [Perfect is the enemy of good]" - Voltaire

Voltaire welcomed us into this together. It is fitting that he should help close us out. The goal here was not to address every single aspect of crisis communications. As I said in the introduction, that would be a tedious and endless bore. The goal was not perfection either. Any attempt to achieve the unattainable would have blurred the greatness we can achieve.

The goal was to provide you enough seeds to grow, enough branches to innovate, and a few blossoms to help you shine. In the end, you choose the tools.

You cultivate your own garden.

I will close out with one last personal story. Have you noticed that when celebrities die, we all react differently? We may have had a personal connection to them, their work, their life, or with how they died. It can feel like the loss of a close friend or family member. I remember my parents, big NASCAR fans, were heartbroken in February 2001, when driver Dale Earnhart crashed and died at Daytona International Speedway. For them, Earnhart *was* NASCAR. They tuned in each weekend to watch him race. The loss was tragic for them.

We all have someone like that who has made an indelible impact. For me, it was Chef Anthony Bourdain, who committed suicide by hanging in 2018. It hit me deeply on a few levels. Long before he passed, I got a tattoo of a semi colon on the back of my right hand, to show support and compassion for people with depression, anxiety, and suicidal thoughts. It was, and is, an issue I care deeply about. In addition, he was only slightly older than me at the time. As you get older you cannot help but compare the lives, choices, and deaths among your generation.

But more than any of that, it was about his book, "Kitchen Confidential," that he published in 2000. I never cooked in my adult life, until I came across his book in 2007. I read it cover to cover in one sitting. I was fascinated and mesmerized. I was inspired. I began cooking that day. I have not become a chef, or even an above-average home cook. In fact, most of my friends are better cooks. But I found a happy place.

If you asked me to summarize the book today, I remember that he told us bchind the scenes stories of the restaurant industry, and many of them were dark and difficult. But beyond that, there are hundreds of pages of his words that I have long forgotten.

But I remember these: Use real butter, choose shallots over onions, and always have some homemade stock on hand. I learned to begin my cooking with *mise en place*. If you read his book, you may have retained other incidental information. And I cherish those morsels.

My wish for you, and me, after reading "Cultivate Your Garden," is merely that you found a crumb, were inspired by a fleck, incorporated a grain, or planted a new seed.

###

About the Author

As a Strategic Communications Consultant, Dan is inspired by the movie "Cool Hand Luke." The character, Captain, tells Paul Newman's character (Luke), "What we've got here is failure to communicate." The irony in that scene is that Captain is complicit in the failure. But he does not know what he does not know. He is not alone. Dan is a strategic communicator. He is a writer. Dan's expertise is born from experience, to include his role at the Pentagon upon the attacks of 9/11; as lead spokesperson for the National Guard in Louisiana during Hurricane Katrina where he represented 54 states and territories; responding to the earthquake in Haiti where he helped establish the first-ever international joint information center; creating a coalition with the private sector to implement the first national business emergency operation center; and voluntarily deploying to Puerto Rico within hours of Hurricane Maria's impact as the lead national and international spokesperson.

Dan has been a soldier, a teacher, a corporate public relations vice president, and a small business owner. He is currently the Founder and Vice President of the Emergency Management External Affairs Association (EMEAA). In addition, Dan is the Owner and Principal at Stoneking Strategic Communications LLC

(SSC). He has extensive experience in leadership counsel, risk/crisis communications, media relations, media training, strategic messaging, branding, public-private partnerships and reputation management.

Graduating from the University of New Hampshire, with a Bachelor's in Interpersonal Communications, he later returned to the same campus and earned a Master of Arts in Teaching (Secondary English). He taught High School English for two years. This is Dan's second book. His first book, "Still in Motion," is a digital collection of poetry and other vignettes, https://www.barnesandnoble.com/w/still-in-motion-dan-stoneking/1143766271 . Dan continues to write on his platform, *Stoneking's Crisis Crib Notes Editorials*, at https://crisiscribnotes.substack.com/ . You can learn more about Dan's vision, philosophy, qualifications, programs and services at his SSC website, www.danstoneking.com

Dan retired from a formal, structured workforce in 2023 and is living life on his terms. He lives in West Chester, PA with his two daughters, Ivy Grace and Chloe Lane.

###

About the Co-Author

Rebecca was born and raised in Southern California. She received her B.A. from Haverford College, outside of Philadelphia, and took courses in fifteen different disciplines. She credits her liberal arts background for being able to make unexpected connections.

After college, she worked with domestic violence survivors before becoming a college admissions officer. She decided to go back to school and was, to her surprise, admitted to the University of Oxford. There, she met her now-husband and received her Master's degree in International Relations. Not ready to stop doing research, she came back to the East Coast to complete a PhD in Women and Politics at Rutgers University. She was an election observer, spoke at the United Nations, interviewed politicians, and taught classes in English and political science.

After her PhD, on a whim, she applied for a job in emergency management. Dan was leading the division. It was because of her interview with Dan that she took the job.

Rebecca lives in Pennsylvania with her husband and daughters. In her spare time--limited with two small children--she likes to travel and cook. And she still loves to learn.

###

– The End –

Printed in Great Britain
by Amazon

38013822R00198